SOCIALIST HIST

SOCIALIST
OCCASIONAL PUBLICATION NO. 37

'STOP THE FIRST WORLD WAR!'

MOVEMENTS OPPOSED TO THE 1914-1918 WAR IN BRITAIN, FRANCE AND GERMANY

KEITH LAYBOURN
DUNCAN BOWIE
HELEN BOAK
IAN BIRCHALL
JOHN S PARTINGTON

ED. DAVID MORGAN

2016

Published by the Socialist History Society 2016

ISBN 978-0-9930104-2-2

Designed and typeset by SHS 2016

Contents

Introduction

The present publication is the outcome of a programme of events held at Conway Hall, Holborn, London, in 2014, the year of the centennial commemoration of the start of the First World War. The series of talks on the overall theme of *Stop the First World War* and the accompanying conference were intended to be contributions from the left to the debate on the historical legacy of the war. In particular, this volume seeks to provide an historical understanding of how patterns of opposition to the war developed over time as the protracted fighting came to be viewed as a futile slaughter. As casualty figures on the battlefields mounted public trust in their political leaders was replaced with scepticism, disdain and anger, while loyalties collapsed towards what was widely perceived as an out-of-touch and incompetent officer class. Such popular sentiments linger on to this day and are perhaps best reflected in powerful anti-war satires such as Joan Littlewood's classic *Oh, What a Lovely War!* which itself was successfully revived at Theatre Royal, Stratford East, in 2014.

While we honour the memory of all those who needlessly fell in the international carnage of 1914-1918, this publication is devoted to the political activists, trade unionists, conscientious objectors, rank-and-file soldiers, daughters, mothers and sisters, who formed part of the opposition to the war. Many of these people did not see themselves as pacifists at all, but were simply individuals who had found themselves pushed to breaking point as the horrific ordeal of the war continued year on year with apparently no end in sight.

It is extremely important to acknowledge that anti-war senti-ments were shared by citizens in all of the nations which were combatants in the conflict. As such the publication's editors are especially pleased to be able to include the essays on anti-war opposition in France and Germany.

Far too much blood has continued to be spilled in wars around the world in the century since the First World War and sadly this continues to be the case. As of the end of 2015, wars are raging on interminably in Syria, Iraq, Afghanistan and Ukraine, all involving exactly the same imperial powers which took the world to the brink in 1914. The international anti-war movement of the early 21st century has perhaps been more persistent in its opposition to these contemporary wars than were its forerunners in the first decades of the last century, a small part of whose activities are documented in this publication.

In organising the talks in 2014 and in this follow up Occasional Publication the Socialist History Society intends to rescue the members of these too often forgotten anti-war movements 'from the enormous condescension of posterity', to cite the frequently quoted words of E P Thompson.

The name of the aforementioned perennially popular drama by Joan Littlewood, which was also made into a celebrated film by Richard Attenborough, inspired the title of the SHS conference, *Not Such A Lovely War*, from which Helen Boak's contribution to this collection derives. Other contributions to the conference included Professor Kevin Morgan whose talk titled 'Class cohesion and spurious patriotism: trade union internationalism in the First World War' is readily available elsewhere in a publication from the Bristol Radical History Group which was supported by the SHS.

The SHS Honorary President and former Labour MP, Stan Newens delivered a talk titled, 'Imperialist Rivalries and the Origins of the First World War', while Keith Flett, Convenor of the London Socialist Historians Group, gave a talk titled, 'So Bloody Much to Oppose - grassroots opposition to World War One'.

Three of the essays included here, namely those by Keith Laybourn, Duncan Bowie and Ian Birchall, were prepared for and delivered in the series of talks. Keith was unfortunately unable to deliver his contribution in person due to illness, but portions of it were read out on his behalf. This is the first time, however, that the full text has been made widely available and it constitutes the longest piece within these pages. John Partington, the co-author of an earlier SHS book on Clara Zetkin, contributes the final essay in this volume. Unlike the rest of the essays this was not specifically written for the talks, but it is included because it fits so well into the overall theme and it more than adequately complements Boak's illuminating article.

In conclusion, the SHS would very much like to thank its friends at the Conway Hall who agreed that it was a good idea to organise the events and generously offered the venue for the talks and the conference.

We extend our thanks also to all of the speakers and participants and would like to express apologies for being unable to publish the excellent contributions in their entirety in this modest volume.

We owe a debt of gratitude to Deborah Lavin, who was the curator of the talks series and who acted as a vital link for the SHS in our productive collaboration with Conway Hall.

Finally, I hope that readers find this volume as enlightening and entertaining as were the original lectures and discussions on which it is based.

David Morgan, on behalf of the Editorial Team

A Movement Divided: the Labour Movement and the Great War — a Divided Bradford and a United Huddersfield

Keith Laybourn

Historians have long recognised that the Great War (1914-1918) was a crucial moment of change in British political history. To Arthur Marwick it damaged the Liberal Party and strengthened the Labour Party.[1] To Trevor Wilson it 'increased the importance of the trade unions and so stimulated their political consciousness that it correspondingly enhanced the position of the Labour Party'.[2] Although the Conservative Party experienced a resurgence of influence during the war, the focus of debate has tended to be placed on the way the war damaged the Liberals and strengthened Labour. Yet at the same time the Great War initially led to deep divisions within the ranks of the Labour movement, between pro-war and anti-war groups, which could have been as debilitating to Labour's growth as it may have been for the Liberal Party, had it not been for the fact that the Labour movement was largely pro-war, that the anti-war members saw themselves as patriotic defenders of civil liberties, and that the introduction of military conscription in 1916 unified the Labour movement behind the War Emergency: Workers' National Committee and its 'conscription of riches' campaign.[3]

The Parliamentary Labour Party famously supported the government's war effort from 5 August 1914, the day after the outbreak of war, though the Independent Labour Party (ILP), which was affiliated to the Labour Representation Committee, was institutionally opposed to war after its 1915 Conference. The ILP's opposition to war was, however, tempered by the fact that the majority of ILP members who were eligible to fight did so even in the textile district of the West Riding of Yorkshire, which was a so-called hotspot of pacifism. The Clarion Movement, the cultural organisation of ethical socialism which emphasised brotherhood and fellowship, was deeply divided on war for, whilst the majority of its members opposed war, Robert Blatchford, its founder, wrote his anti-German book *General von Sneak: A little study of war* and maintained a pro-war position in the *Clarion* along with Edward Robertshaw Hartley, the Bradford butcher who was the organiser of the Clarion Van movement, a member of the ILP and the British Socialist Party (BSP).[4] Famously, the quasi-Marxist BSP, which had emerged from the Socialist Democratic Federation and the Social Democratic Party, was divided between the pro-war attitude of the old guard, including Henry Mayers Hyndman, and the new guard of internationalists, led by Zelda Kahan, which favoured peace. Indeed, the BSP held five regional conferences in February 1915. In Glasgow and London, the opponents of war held the upper hand, but it was those in favour of the Great War who prevailed elsewhere. The situation worsened when, following the Conference of Allied Socialists in London, the Allied Internationalists met at Zimmerwald in September 1915 to reconstruct the Second International of reformist socialist groups, which had collapsed on the outbreak of war. The resulting Zimmerwald Manifesto blamed imperialism and capitalist greed for the Great War and advocated that all socialist nations should fight for peace.[5] Hyndman rejected this but the internationalists accepted it, although Kahan was unclear about how this objective was to be achieved. The BSP pro-war sections then began to join groups such as the Socialist National Defence Committee, which became the British Workers' League before becoming the National Democratic Party. These pro-war bodies attracted other patriotic socialists such as A. M. Thompson and Blatchford, from the *Clarion*, and Hartley, Dan Irving, Bert Killip, Ben Tillett, J. J. Terrett and Will Thorne of the BSP. Some members of the Labour Party also joined them. Hyndman gave his support, if not his membership to them, but he, like many other figures, eventually dissociated himself from the National Democratic Party.

Thus there is a conundrum: how was it that a divided Labour movement emerged from the Great War in better shape than a divided Liberal Party to dominate progressive politics in inter war Britain? The frequently expressed explanation, exemplified by the work of Trevor Wilson, that it was the war alone that destroyed Liberal values and favoured the growth of the Labour Party is far too simplistic and does not allow for the difficulties that war clearly posed for a Labour movement which had increasingly been raised on the concept of international brotherhood. Indeed, it will be argued here, that the answer is problematic and nuanced but probably involves three main developments in the Great War which merged to favour the Labour movement's post-war growth. The first is the blindingly obvious point that, despite deep divisions, the Labour movement as a whole was overwhelmingly patriotic and that even the membership of its officially pacifist and anti-war sections, and particularly the ILP, was clearly patriotic. This was the case in 'pacifist Bradford' and even the case in Huddersfield, which Cyril Pearce has dubbed a 'community of conscience' because of the number of conscientious objectors it produced in a town that was apparently sympathetic towards pacifists.[6] Secondly, the introduction of military conscription in January 1916 through the Military Services Act reunited the fissured Labour movement in its desire to see the war brought to a speedy, possibly negotiated, conclusion, despite the differences in attitude towards the war. Thirdly, the Labour movement was galvanised by the formation of the War Emergency: Workers' National Committee (WEWNC) which, as Royden Harrison, Paul Ward and J. M. Winter have noted, united more than a hundred Labour organisations to promote neutrality and peace on 5 August 1914, but which, with Parliamentary Labour Party immediately throwing its hand in with the Asquith wartime government, changed direction to work for the improvement of the lot of working-class families faced with enormous wartime rent and food rises.[7] The one issue that unified these disparate and fractious labour and socialist groups in the WEWNC was the 'conscription of riches' campaign which promoted the initially vague, undeveloped, commitment to public ownership of the means of production which eventually became the major ideological and socialist feature of the Labour Party's 1918 Constitution, the famous 'Clause IV'. Collectively, then, a Labour movement, even though divided by war, was able to maintain some type of unity.

A divided nation and the Labour movement

The anguish of the Labour movement over the Great War was part of a wider disquiet among the progressive movement. Only the Conservative and Unionist Party, bitterly divided about its future and leadership from 1911 onwards, seems to have benefited politically from the war. Overwhelmingly nationalistic, and thus indubitably patriotic, drawn into the Wartime Coalition Government of Asquith in May 1915, and partly responsible for David Lloyd George replacing Asquith as Prime Minister in 1916, it prospered politically from war. On the other hand, the Liberal Party was deeply divided. The likes of John Henry of Leeds and C. P. Trevelyan, Liberal MP for Elland in Yorkshire, were horrified at the outbreak of war and wanted an immediate cessation of hostilities. The Prime Minister, H. H. Asquith, wished for an international settlement, whilst Lloyd George, the pacifist of the Boer War, wanted nothing less than outright victory and was depicted as a 'war-monger'. From the start, the Labour movement very closely resembled the position of the Liberal Party with strong support for the war but with significant and voluble groups of opposition. On the one hand, many middle-class and working-class socialist activists joined with other progressives to oppose war. However, the majority of the trade-union base of the Labour Party, united by the Trade Union Congress, overwhelmingly supported the war effort through the Treasury Agreement of 1915, which guaranteed the return to their jobs of male workers who had gone to fight. Indeed, because of the labour shortage in war wages increased and, with better pay, workers were able to join unions and trade union membership increased from about six millions in 1916 to about 6.5 millions in 1918, and to eight millions by 1920. Initially, then, the Labour movement was, like other movements, unprepared for war.

The outbreak of war in August 1914 had come with startling suddenness, despite the fact that there had been considerable socialist opposition to war on the eve of war. Reverend R. Roberts, a Congregational Minister in Bradford and a member of the ILP, was not untypical of many socialists when he expressed his moral outrage against a threatened war in early 1914:

> Alone amongst the parties of Great Britain the Labour Party is pledged against militarism... We must take up the Fiery Cross and carry it to the remotest hamlet in the country, call every man and woman to the colours. 'Down with militarism'. That is our cry – as it also the cry of our comrades all over Europe. Blazon it on the banners. Write it on the pavements. Sing it in the streets.[8]

As late as 1 August 1914, continental socialist leaders were still convinced that war was not a possibility. However, as Georges Haupt suggests, they were captives of their own myths about their ability to prevent war and unaware of the depths of national chauvinism. Apparently, they were then cut short by the events, pushed on the defensive and became disorientated spectators, waiting to be submerged by the gathering wave of nationalism.

Very quickly both the political and economic sides of the wider Labour movement became divided. In addition, James Ramsay MacDonald, Secretary of the Labour Party and the most powerful of Britain's Labour leaders, resigned when the Labour Party (actually the Parliamentary Labour Party) decided to support the Asquith government's pursuit of the war on 5 August 1914, objecting to the secret treaties that had led to war. He was replaced by Arthur Henderson who took the Labour Party into the Wartime Coalition in May 1915 though Henderson was finally removed from his Cabinet position in the famous 'doorstep' incident, where he was asked to wait outside the office of the Prime Minister because of his more pacific views after his visit to revolutionary Russia in 1917, before resigning.

The ILP, which was affiliated to the Labour Party, officially opposed the war at its 1915 Conference but quickly divided into four groups, a spectrum ranging from pacifists to patriots. The first group were the pacifists, and included Clifford Allen, J. Bruce Glasier, Arthur Salter, Fenner Brockway, and, on the fringe, Philip Snowden though he was not a fully committed pacifist.[10] The second group felt the need to protect Britain and protect Belgium whilst opposing the secret treaties that led to war and supporting calls for peace. The third group felt that the need to prosecute the war was essential to the defence of the country and temporarily transcended socialist objectives. The fourth group, closely allied with the third group, felt that Prussianism was the real danger to the world and had to be defeated come what may. Such divisions were, as previously indicated, evident within the ranks of the BSP, where Hyndman's nationalists conflicted with Kahan's internationalists. The Clarion movement continued to be dominated by anti-war socialists who disowned Robert Blatchford.

Yet at the same time one must bear in mind that reactions to the war were complex and refracted through an individual's racial, religious, class, gender and occupational identity. Thus, for example, an Irish Catholic's support for the war was always going to be shaped and coloured by the 'Irish question' – the issue of Home Rule or independence for Ireland. Similarly, a labour activist who had sought to foster international bonds of solidarity with the working classes of other countries – including Germany – opposed the war through the prism of their own social and class position.

While many felt a sense of duty to support the British Empire in times of crisis, this did not obliterate alternative loyalties, and many felt a conflict of these loyalties during the war. On the whole, however, even when the war situation appeared to be getting worse after the stalemates of the 1916-1917 offensives – the battle of Verdun, the Somme and Passchendaele – and the increased shortages of the home front, the British populace and wider Empire remained loyal to the war. There was not the revolutionary ferment of Russia or anything like the mutiny of French troops in 1917.

For the minority who opposed the war, religious, gender, race, class and occupational identities clearly shaped their ideas and associations. The pacifists, those who opposed all war, drew in socialists, such as Sylvia Pankhurst, intellectual pacifists such as the novelist Virginia Woolf, Bertrand Russell, Ottoline Morrell and the Garsington set, who operated closely with conscientious objectors, and activists such as Norman Angell, who was later to win the Nobel Peace Prize for his pacifist book *The Great Illusion*. In addition, many members of the ILP, like James Keir Hardie and Fred Jowett, opposed the Great War specifically because of the secret treaties that had led to it. They intermingled with organisations such as the Union of Democratic Control (UDC) and the League of Nations Union who reflected an upswing in the belief in future arbitration to prevent war and drew upon the support of serving men and women fighting in the 'war to end all wars'. Many of these people and groups were derided as cowards or as traitors – Bertrand Russell was, for instance, dismissed from his post at Cambridge. After the war, however, many of them had their reputations rehabilitated – the general feeling after the losses of the war was one of a need to find peaceful solutions to conflict in the future through international arbitration – and there was a groundswell of support for the new League of Nations. Most of these groups contained fascinating individuals with complex responses to war. However, the focus here is targeted at Labour and socialist groups and in order to illustrate these divisions within the Labour movement it is instructive to look particularly at the Bradford Labour movement, which was inaccurately presented by the large sections of the press and some politicians as being anti-war.

War and the Labour Movement in Bradford: Pacifist, Anti-War and Pro-War views before and after Military Conscription in 1916

Bradford was a centre of Labour growth from the late nineteenth and early twentieth centuries following the bitter and protracted nineteen-week Manningham Mills strike of 1890-1, out of which the Bradford Labour Union/ILP emerged. It was in Bradford that the National ILP developed to dominate the early Labour movement, even after the Labour Representation Committee and the Labour Party emerged. It was here where a Workers' Municipal Federation (WMF), formed at the turn of the century to establish a Labour presence on the local city council, linking the ILP and the Labour Party, with the Bradford Trades and Labour Council (who established it). By 1913 the ILP/Labour/WMF group was receiving 43.1 per cent of the municipal vote, though their political ambitions were checked by a Conservative-Liberal anti-socialist alliance, and had one of Bradford's three MPs – Fred Jowett who was returned for Bradford West in 1906.[11] It was at St. George's Hall in Bradford (the birthplace of the national ILP) that the 21st 'Coming of Age' Conference of the ILP was held in April 1914. Bradford was thus a centre of Labour growth in the quarter of a century before the Great War.

Between 1912 and 1914 there were many articles in the *Bradford Pioneer,* the local Independent Labour Party newspaper, representing the views of the burgeoning Bradford Labour movement on the Armaments Trust, the secret diplomacy, and the need to foster international unity. These exhibited a commitment to internationalism rather than steps to stop war. On the eve of war the Bradford Labour movement vehemently expressed its opposition to conflict and called for a simultaneous stoppage of work in those countries where war was threatened. In the midst of a period of national ultimatums, the ILP held a mass meeting on 2 August 1914 which deplored the threatened war but which did not advocate immediate working-class action to avoid it. In his speech to this meeting, Fred Jowett ILP MP for Bradford West, and a once prominent member of the Trades Council, spoke of the need to bring peace through a common socialism and quoted from Bradford Trades Council's anti-war resolution of 1912

> ...of the proposal for a general stoppage of work in all countries about to engage in war, and further we urge upon all workers the necessity for making preparations for a simultaneous stoppage of work in those countries where was is threatened.[12]

He argued that war was 'a crime against humanity' but made no calls for strikes or mass demonstrations to oppose it. Rather he closed his speech with a note of resignation: 'Let us who are socialists keep in our minds calm, our hearts free from hate, and one purpose always before us – to bring peace as soon as possible on a basis that will endure.'[13]

Such sentiments became rarer after the declaration of war. Very quickly both the ethical and trade-union elements of the Bradford Labour Party divided into anti-war and pro-war factions, though this was far more obvious within the ILP, which dominated the local Labour Party. The impression was given by the local, as well as national, press that the ILP, in particular, was opposed to war and unpatriotic. Indeed, shortly after the National ILP had passed a resolution opposing war, in 1915, the *Bradford Weekly Telegraph* wrote of the ILP's inability to 'raise a single finger to help the country to prosecute the war successfully'. Jowett replied to this by stating that 'In proportion to its membership the ILP had more adherents serving in the army and navy by far than either of the other two political parties.'[14] Nonetheless, the *Bradford Weekly Telegraph* continued with its criticism in July 1915 stating that

> Considering how bravely our manhood is serving the state of Flanders, if these demagogues [ILP] lack the spine to fight the least they should do would be to remain silent and inactive whilst others do the nation's work.[15]

However, local censuses of the Bradford ILP membership confirm that Jowett was right. One census conducted in February 1916 indicated that of 461 young men, in the local ILP party membership of 1473, 113 were in the trenches, four had been killed, one was missing, nine had been wounded, three were prisoners of war 118 were training in England, six were in the navy and 207 were attested under the Derby scheme as necessary home workers.[16] Another census in 1918 found that of the 492 members liable to service 351 were serving in the forces whilst 48 were conscientious objectors or were in national work.[17]

The impression that the Bradford ILP was a party of pacifists was simply an illusion created by a press which failed to understand that, despite the ILP Conference's pacifist resolution of 1915, the ILP, like the Quakers, acknowledged individual conscience and was equivocal on the war. Jowett himself, indeed, opposed the war at the same time as he honoured those of the ILP who fought or died in war – a position also assumed by Keir Hardie, the national Labour leader who in August 1914 had said that 'the lads who have gone forth to fight their country's battles must not be disheartened by any discordant notes at home.'[18] There were complex reasons and associations operating within the socialist and Labour movement in Bradford refracted in the light of personal experiences. Almost all of the Bradford ILP men of an eligible age fought for their country though many did so in the hope of winning a lasting post-war peace. Indeed, the *Bradford Pioneer* offered a further insight into this relationship between the so-called pacific ILP and the boys at the front by publishing a letter to Jowett from a soldier in France.

> Dear Mr. Jowett,
> As one of 'the Boys' allow me to thank you personally for your efforts for peace during the past four years. I am quite sure that when 'the Boys' come home they will give you the TRUTH, re the terrible wastage of lives, inhuman conditions, filth and immoral environ-

11

ment, and thus you will live in the memories of YOUNG men as being a MAN of whom we can be justly proud. I hope that you will be returned at the head of the poll on the 14th December. [This was a reference to the coming 1918 General Election.]

A Boy from France.[19]

The fact is that the Bradford ILP, and the Bradford Labour movement as a whole, adopted a range of positions on war, although the vast majority were pro-war but tolerant of the views of others.

There were, indeed, few ILP pacifists at the national level but they did include Clifford Allen, Bruce Glasier, Arthur Salter, Fenner Brockway and Philip Snowden, from Keighley. They were largely middle-class members of the ILP and were frequently involved in the formation of the Union of Democratic Control (UDC) in 1914, which was not a pacifist organisation but sought a reasoned foreign policy, free of military influence (though it later also opposed military conscription). The UDC formed by E. D. Morel, supported by Sir John Simon and many of his Liberal colleagues, and many of its members, both Liberal and Labour, were later in the war drawn into the No-Conscription Fellowship. The main Bradford pacifist was Willie Leach, an employer who had joined the Bradford ILP in 1895. He wrote for *Bradford Labour Echo* (in the mid 1890s) and *Forward* (from about 1900 to 1906) and took over from the pro-war Joseph Burgess, the man who called the socialists together to form the National ILP in Bradford, as editor of the *Bradford Pioneer*. In October 1915, Leach articulated the paper's policy

> We hate all war especially the present one. This is a pacifist and peace journal conducted among other purposes with the object of stating as well as we can, the ILP position on the hideous tragedy now being enacted in Europe.... Human life is the most sacred thing we know and its preservation, its development, its best welfare, must therefore be our religion on this earth.[20]

However, the Bradford pacifists saw themselves as a beleaguered group, led by William Leach who, through the *Bradford Pioneer,* reported extensively on the No-Conscription Fellowship and the UDC (the No-Conscription Fellowship caught on well West Yorkshire as indicated in Table 1) and the speeches of pacifists and anti-war figures who spoke at the New Picture House in Morley Street. The *Pioneer* described E. D. Morel who lectured there as 'that distinguished war bird... now a member of the ILP and of the Bradford Branch'.[21] Leach, through the *Bradford Pioneer*, was also concerned at the attack on Germans in Bradford, most Germanized town in

Britain with its middle-class families of German origin such as the Mosers, the Wolffs, the Behrens, the Steinthals, and the Delius family.

Leach's pacifist views were supported by a small group of trade unionists and political figures in Bradford, including Walter Barber, Secretary of the Bradford Trades Council, and his son Revis Barber, who became one of the estimated 59 Conscientious Objectors (COs) (see Table 2) in Bradford who refused to be conscripted from 1916 onwards, though we now know that there likely to be more.[22]

At the end of the war William Leach stood for Bradford Central, where he was comprehensively defeated by the Conservative Coalition candidate. Yet he reiterated his commitment to pacifism:

> I have never felt so pugnaciously right in my life. I still disbelieve in war. As long as I am in public life I will not support bloodshed for any cause, whether that cause appears right or does not. It looks as if this victory fervour has swept us out. But it will pass. Liberalism is defunct, Socialism is deferred, and the Coalition will be defeated.[23]

Such sentiments were not shared by the majority of the Bradford ILP/Labour Party, nor by many contributors to the *Bradford Pioneer*.

The majority anti-war ILPers in Bradford were not pacifists and were prepared to see the war through. Fred Jowett was amongst them and though opposed to the secret treaties that led to the Great War, favoured the defence of Britain, opposed Prussianism but as the *Standard* wrote 'His fad was the democratic control of foreign policy', and he wanted the 'restoration of Belgium to complete sovereignty'.[24] This was something akin to Keir Hardie's, 'We must see the War through, but denounce Secret Diplomacy.'[25] Jowett was opposed to the secret treaties and he combined this with the idea of National Defence being voted upon by Parliament. Indeed at the 1915 ILP Conference, when the ILP passed a resolution opposing the war, he stated that 'Now is the time to speak and ensure that never again shall the witches' cauldron of secret diplomacy brew the broth of Hell for mankind.'[26] As Chairman of the ILP Conference in 1916 he reflected on the ILP anti-war resolution (of 1915) that there was a difference between the commitment of a movement and the commitment of an individual:

> I believe that the war would never have arisen if the government had carried out an open and honest foreign policy and disclosed to the people who had most to lose in the relations between themselves and foreign governments with whom they are acting in collusion.

[....] The ILP resolution to which you refer only expressed the view that Socialist Parties as organised bodies should support no war. It did not attempt to lay down such a policy for individuals. If it did I should be opposed to it in principle.

Jowett was acknowledging that the majority of the ILP members in Bradford were committed to the Great War on the grounds of National Defence and in the belief that Prussianism had to be destroyed. Also, by the middle of August 1914 the Rev. R. Roberts, who had, two weeks before, taken up the 'Fiery Cross' against war had totally changed his position and was now stating that:

...the hour of reckoning had come. The legend of 'blood and iron' has to be shattered. Either it must be smashed or civilisation must go under. Its victory would be the enthronement of the War God in the centre of European civilization and the crushing of Socialism for generations.27

Two months later he added that he had fought for peace for forty years in public life but that:

We are threatened with the 'ruin of civilised society' and that 'At whatever cost of life and treasure we must fight. I cannot tell the pain it cost me to write that sentence. I never thought I should live to do it.'...Better to die than be Prussianised. Better to be wiped off the face of the earth than to exist squealing and squirming under the Prussian jack boots.28

This type of view was strongly held by many other members of the ILP.

The two leading pro-war figures in Bradford Labour politics were Joseph Burgess and Edward Robertshaw Hartley. Burgess was a newspaper man who had had a long association with the ILP. It was his newspaper, *The Workman's Times*, which had called together delegates from Labour societies to meet at a conference in Bradford in January 1893, at which the National Independent Labour Party had been formed. He was a member of the Socialist Sunday School movement, editor of the *Yorkshire Factory Times,* was later editor of the *Bradford Pioneer* until the summer of 1915 and was elected President of the Bradford ILP in 1915. At first a critic of war he proclaimed that 'we have no quarrel with Germany ... Stand firm workers to those who would appeal to you in the name of patriotism.' However, he changed his position in 1915, joined the Socialist National Defence Committee, whose motto was 'Britain for the British' a slogan coined by Robert Blatchford, in June 1915 and was threatening to stand as a parliamentary candidate for the National

Socialist Party in Blackburn (against Philip Snowden) although he never did so. There was a flurry of critical letters in the *Bradford Pioneer,* and responses by Burgess, in what was dubbed the 'Burgess Comedy'.[29] Burgess influenced the Bradford Socialist Sunday School and, in association with the Leeds Armley Socialist School, even attempted, albeit unsuccessfully, to overturn the Yorkshire Union of Socialist Sunday Schools anti-war position.[30] He left the Labour movement and later moved to Scotland to edit newspapers before making his return to Labour politics in the late 1920s.[31]

Edward Robertshaw Hartley's patriotism was similarly divisive. He was a butcher by trade and in the 1890s and early twentieth century, because of his singing activities, was frequently described as 'a butcher who gave renderings'. He had been a member of the SDF but it was weak in Bradford, rarely having more than about 25 members or so in the 1890s and swinging in and out of existence, and so he joined the ILP in the mid 1890s. He was a Bradford City councillor and was ILP candidate in East Bradford for the parliamentary seat in 1906 and 1910. He was also a prominent figure in the Clarion Movement and is often seen in photos on the seat of the Van or orating from it at the side of his daughter, Gertrude. Having travelled abroad in 1913 he was, on his return, immediately parachuted into the Dewsbury parliamentary by-election in 1913 for the British Socialist Party. The ILP objected to this but Hartley retained some ILP support in his old Bradford Moor ward. At the beginning of the Great War he had adopted a pro-war stance, anticipated the introduction of military conscription, and became the pro-war British Workers' League (BWL) in the Bradford area.[32] At its inaugural meeting at Whetley Lane, Bradford there were about 1,000 people present, three-quarters of whom, it was reflected, were hostile to his stand.[33] A. Howarth of the BWL, stated of the Bradford ILP and the war 'Bradford has disgraced itself more than any other town in the country.'[34] Victor Fisher, an old SDF/SDP/BSP figure, who had become secretary of the BWL, stated before a Bradford audience that 'Sinister pacifism is more rampant in your midst than in any other part of the United Kingdom with the exception of perhaps the Clyde and South Wales.'[35] However, sinister or not, the opposition to the war, if not pacifism, was about to increase.

The position of the Bradford Trade Unionists, Conscription, and the War Emergency: Workers' National Committee from 1916 onwards

On January 1916 the Military Services Act brought military conscription to Britain for the first time. Six months later, on 1 July, 57,000 British soldiers were killed or injured on the first day of the Battle of the Somme, a battle which eventually cost 1,000,000 deaths or injuries to the horror and all and further raised issues in Britain about the settlement of the war.[36] It has been described by Max Hastings as 'the great betrayal of innocents – and of the old working class in khaki – by Britain's ruling classes in breeches and glossy riding boots', in his sweeping attack upon incompetent generals who sent brave and naive soldiers to their deaths.[37] Field Marshall Haig's suggestion that this five-month battle would be the 'decisive' battle proved to be futile and one of indiscriminate slaughter which shook the foundations of pre-war British society and may have contributed in a significant way to loosening the bounds which constrained class politics. Centrally, however, the introduction of conscription transformed the young men of military age who opposed the war into criminals or 'prisoners of conscience'. Many of them were from the same ideological roots and organisational communities which had driven Labour on to become a party of government.

Most trade unionists in Bradford were initially supporters of the war effort – though that dominance declined as the war progressed. Trade unionists such as Jessie Cockerline, also a member of the ILP, wrote an article 'My Country Right or Wrong' in the *Bradford Pioneer,* 14 August 1914. Other supporters of the war included J. H. Palin and A. W. Brown, both prominent members of the ILP. The fact is that the Bradford Trades and Labour Council (BTLC) was just as divided over the war as the ILP and the Labour Party.

Jessie Cockerline and J. H. Palin were keenly patriotic. Palin was chairman of the Amalgamated Society of Railway Servants as the time of Taff Vale, an ILP councillor and alderman in Bradford and trade union correspondent of the *Bradford Pioneer,* and had chaired the 21st Conference of the ILP held at Bradford in 1914. At the 1916 National ILP Conference he had bluntly stated that 'we do not want Germans here'. He then went off to France to help with war transportation, returned to continue his career in Labour politics and became Labour MP for one of the Newcastle seats in the 1920s.

The Trades Council was opposed to war before 1914. In November 1912, the BTLC passed a resolution committing it to a general stoppage in the case of a war. The 'Anglo-German War' or 'European War', however, caught the Trades Council unawares. It did not call the general stoppage it had vowed to do, and it drifted into the Labour Party policy of working with the Government. In 1914 and 1915 it was dealing with the practical realities of war - anti-rent raising campaigns, checking on famine prices and food shortages, providing pensions to war widows as part of the duties of the War Emergency: Workers' National Committee. But the BTLC was the litmus paper to the changing mood of the Bradford working class and the Left in Bradford as a whole. The silent majority gave their tacit support for the war but a small group of activists – George Licence, Charlie Glyde and J. W. Ormandroyd – opposed it, supported by other ILP and trade-union and ILP activists such as Fred Jowett. There were clear divisions with the pro-war section predominating. However, with the risk of military conscription emerging in 1915, things began to change and conscription proved pivotal. In June 1915 the BTLC passed a resolution

...believing conscription in any form to be a violation of the principle of civic freedom hitherto prized as one of the chief heritages of British liberty, and that its adoption would constitute a grave menace to the progress of the nation; it believes that a recourse to a compulsory system is uncalled for in view of the enormous roll of enlistments since the war began and further; it is impossible to reconcile a national service in industry with private profit-making, and further protests against those employers who are dismissing men because they are of military age. It therefore urges Parliament to offer their utmost opposition to any proposal to impose upon the British people a yoke which is one of the chief concerns of Prussian militarism.[38]

The concern expressed here was also just as much with the Munitions Act of 1915, which had suspended 'trade union rights' and prevented vital workers moving from job to job without a certificate of approval from their employer, as it was against military conscription. Yet the threat of military conscription caused the main reaction as it was discussed in 1915. Gradually, the BTLC found that it began to drift away from the TUC parliamentary circular calling for trade union help in army recruitment and, in a series of votes, slowly moved to an anti-war position in 1915. A vote in November 1915 indicated a more or less equal split of opinion but another, following a BTLC circular in December 1915, responded to by a third of the affiliated societies, had 19 affiliated societies with 6,757 members voting against supporting army recruitment campaigns and 11 societies, with 11,157 wishing to continue to do so. Many small societies did not vote on the matter and three abstained.[39] This measure of opinion changed nothing but the introduction of conscription in January 1916 led to a dramatic decision by the BTLC to withdraw from supporting the army recruitment campaign. Shortly afterwards BTLC organised a Peace Conference which decisively condemned the Labour MPs for joining the Government and pushed strongly for peace negotiations.

The 'peace movement' soon became prevalent within the Trades Council, though there was still a sizeable commitment to the war effort by many affiliated unions. However, it must be remembered that most of those committed to the Peace Campaign were not pacifists, nor opponents of the war, so much as opponents of the Government's military conscription policy which challenged the civil liberties of the nation which they were so patriotically defending. The imprisonment of Revis Barber, the son of Walter Barber who was Secretary of the Trades Council, as a CO also did much to win over more support to the new 'peace movement'.[40]

The Bradford Trades and Labour Council pressured the Yorkshire Federation of Trade Councils to hold a No-Conscription Conference at the Textile Hall, Bradford, in December 1916 and it sent delegates to the ILP No-Conscription Conference held at Leeds. As the BTLC annual report indicated, there were still 'differences of opinion on the Great War' but it was clear that the anti-war position was burgeoning. In 1917 William Leach, editor of the *Bradford Pioneer,* presented his pacifist views to the Trades Council, a peace conference was held on BTLC premises and the BTLC sent delegates to the national formation meeting of the Workers' and Soldiers' Council in Leeds in June 1917, to join the 1,000 and more delegates demanding peace and exclaiming 'Hail the Russian Revolution'. In September 1917 the BTLC affiliated to the broadly anti-war UDC. Thus by 1917 Bradford had become one of the centres of the anti-war movement, although geared more towards an early settlement of conflict, and the BTLC had become one of its chief supporters. Indeed, by 1917 the Trades Council it was being dominated by what the pro-war Palin dubbed 'militant pacifists' though the majority of its members were driven on by anti-conscription feelings rather than pacifist ideas.[41] Yet divided, though it was, over war in both political and industrial organisation, the Bradford Labour movement retained links and a common cause.

The Tory and Liberal press attack upon the Labour 'Peace Movement' was clearly wrong. Bradford may have been a 'hot-bed of pacifism and anti-war feelings' led by the ILP and the Trades Council but there was overwhelmingly strong support for the war effort between 1914 and 1916 which did not evaporate until the Military Conscription Act of January 1916. Even then, there were deep divisions within the movement as evident in the debate in 1914 and 1915. Even after 1916, when military conscription had been introduced, the emphasis remained one of loyalty to the war effort whilst advocating moves towards peace, driven on perhaps by the decimation of the 'Bradford Pals', the two active volunteer regiments of about 2,000 men who fought on the first day of the Battle of the Somme, 1 July 1916, when 1,770 were killed or injured in what proved to be one of the worst days ever for the British army.[42]

From this scenario emerges the vision of a Britain, a British Left and a Bradford Left, committed to the war and the defence of Belgium, in the first couple of years of the war. However, the idea of patriotism being replaced by cynicism by 1916, very much encouraged by some of the post-war memoirs and diaries that were published and most notably by Robert Graves's, *Goodbye To All That,* would appear to be exaggerated. Paul Ward's article on women knitting for the war and with David Taylor's various essays, and recent book, on Patrick MacGill, suggest the continuing faith of many and an underlying patriotism for a country called Britain at the time as there was a longing for peace.[43] The evidence of the Bradford trade union movement tends to confirm this view. Conscription might have changed the balance of opinion amongst Bradford trade unionists towards a negotiated peace but it did still allow for the pro-war and anti-war groups to work in a harmony of types in a situation where it might first appear that the pacifists and anti-war sections were dominating.

This sense of cohesion and balance was also maintained by the fact that there had also been a Bradford branch of the War Emergency: Workers' National Committee from 1914 onwards. Its meetings dealt with wage levels, price increases, food, rents and others issues and their records deal with the minutia of life in the Great War. It was organised by the Trades Council, and the ILP, Labour Party, and many other socialist organisations gathered to it.[44] This, as at the national level, kept the various sections of Bradford Labour operating together and confirms the views of J. M. Winter, Paul Ward and Royden Harrison that there was an underlying unity within the Labour movement despite divisions over the Great War.[45]

19

Conscientious Objectors, Huddersfield and the Great War[46]

In the light of the Bradford Labour movement's essential patriotism driven towards seeking a negotiated settlement of the Great War after 1916, where then does Cyril Pearce's work on nearby Huddersfield as a 'community of resistance' or a 'community of conscience', fit into a picture of widespread labour support for the war? If Pearce is right, the pacifist and anti-war ideas were widely accepted by both the Labour movement and the wider community in Huddersfield, and reflected upon established networks between the Liberal elite, popular support and the Labour and socialist movement in Huddersfield.

Yet from the start, and despite Pearce's insistence upon the preponderance of anti-war feelings in Huddersfield during the Great War, Huddersfield experienced many of the dislocating and extraordinary features of home front life: it sent volunteers, and later conscripts, to fight at the front – indeed up to about 98 per cent of those who could go to war. Those who died are commemorated on the war memorials in Greenhead Park. It nursed the wounded in newly-established war hospitals, including Storthes Hall, which was also a mental hospital. It employed large numbers of women in nursing and industry, although like Bradford there had always been a large number of women employed in textiles. The town took in Belgian refugees fleeing from German occupation. It was also typical in experiencing diverse and complex attitudes to war in general and on this war in particular. Attitudes in Huddersfield ranged from full support of the British government's declaration of war, to objection to war and especially conscription – but a willingness to serve out of loyalty, to, extreme hostility to war on principle, and a refusal to co-operate with the military or war industries at any level.

In many ways, therefore, Huddersfield, like Bradford, serves as a microcosm of the complexities of national responses to the war with divided opinion and competing loyalties. Yet the strength of the pacifist element also makes it stand out. This makes it difficult to use Huddersfield as a representative example of national tends. The strength of opposition to war in Huddersfield thus means that one must be careful to draw any general conclusions on the extent of opposition to the war. However, Pearce argues that one has to examine the ideals that motivated the expression of opposition to war and the links or networks that existed between different pacifist groups to reveal the picture of mutual support (and at times divergence) between different local groups that reflect the ideological and organisational alliances and splits that existed at national level.

He thus dispenses with the notion of pacifists and conscientious objectors as lone individuals acting out the dictates of their personal conscience. Instead, Pearce offers us a view of opposition to the war arising from deep-seated social and political roots which appealed to a large number of people of traditional labour and liberal sympathies. It is these beliefs that Pearce feels largely accounts for the level of opposition in Huddersfield to the war and explain why in Huddersfield there was none of the beatings and public humiliations of pacifists that was a feature of life for the COs elsewhere in the country.

Pearce sees three main areas of opposition to the Great War in Huddersfield. First, there were the traditional old Gladstonian Liberals who subscribed to the ideal of international relations based upon what Gladstone himself termed 'moral' foreign policy, which required conciliation rather than aggression, international arbitration in the case of a dispute between nations, and a ban on war purely to conquer territory. Only when Germany invaded – and by all accounts violated – neutral Belgium did Liberal support for the war emerge. Even then Arthur Sherwell, the Liberal MP for Huddersfield, could not find it in his way to remain within the Liberal wartime government and left the party to sit as an independent Liberal. The Liberal-dominated Town Council was loyal to the Liberal wartime government but this was tempered by a refusal to compromise its traditional Liberal stance including a refusal to suspend council workers to encourage them to 'volunteer' for the army.

Secondly, Pearce feels that there was a broad based popular opposition which took in the ordinary Liberal voters, local feminists, Quakers, some Baptists and Methodists. They were drawn, with others, into the Huddersfield Council of Civil Liberties, the local branch of the Union of Democratic Control, and eventually the No-Conscription Fellowship. Thirdly, there was the local Labour movement, which, unlike the national Labour movement and the Bradford Labour movement, appears to have been overwhelmingly united in its opposition towards the war. The local BSP, organised by Arthur Gardiner, was totally opposed to the war as was the ILP and the majority of the Labour Party and the Trades Council.

This general opposition to the Great War was strengthened by the introduction of military conscription in 1916. Resistance to the introduction of conscription in the autumn of 1915 brought out a solidarity in the West Yorkshire movement which the first year of the war seemed to have undermined. The machinery of conscription after January 1916 – Tribunal hearings, arrests, magistrates courts appearances, reports of Court Martial and the story of the ill-treatment of COs created a narrative of resistance around which the movement united. Many Huddersfield 117 COs (107 in Table 2 but raised to 117 in Table 4) were members of the ILP, BSP or trade-union activists. The most notable example was Arthur Gardiner, a member of the BSP and a trade union leader, who was brought before the Huddersfield Tribunal in March 1916. He became an overnight symbol of resistance to the Great War. Not a middle-class intellectual or a religious opponent of war he was an ethical opponent of the War. The *Leeds Weekly Citizen,* a Labour paper which had been scathing of religious and ethical COs passing through the Leeds Tribunal, welcomed him as a genuine CO who was worthy of Labour support.[47]

Pearce might well be right that in Huddersfield we have an example of an area which was not divided on the war but united in its opposition to war. Nevertheless, the majority who were called up (about 98 per cent) to fight went and fought if they were accepted for the army, even though, as Huddersfield which had the highest proportion of COs related to the nominal manpower available to fight in the various textile areas of the West Riding of Yorkshire, the recognised hot-spot of resistance to the Great War, as indicated in Table 3, with 117 COs at the last count. Against this we have to accept that whilst there was less vilification of COs and opponents of war, the vast majority of the rest went and fought, died, and were memorialised in Huddersfield. Both conscience and patriotism were recognised in Huddersfield which, like the rest of the country, began to move towards the idea of a negotiated peace. Perhaps Huddersfield, and its Labour movement, was less divided over the Great War than Bradford and many other areas of the United Kingdom, but it is clear that the vast majority of those who were conscripted fought for their country.

Table 1
No-Conscription Fellowship Branches in West Yorkshire 1915 and 1916.[48]

Branch	6 May 1915	27 May 1916	1916
Bradford	Yes	Yes	Yes
Bingley		Yes	Yes
Brighouse		Yes	Yes
Halifax	Yes	Yes	Yes
Huddersfield	Yes	Yes	Yes
Keighley & Dist.	Yes	Yes	Yes
Leeds	Yes	Yes	Yes
Mytholmroyd		Yes	Yes
Wakefield	Yes	Yes	Yes

Table 2
The Proportion of COs per 1,000 males eligible for war in some West Riding of Yorkshire towns.[49]

Local authority (1911 Census)	COs	FAU	COs per 000 males
Batley MB	2	1	0.12
Bradford CB	59	8	0.44
Brighouse MB	3	3	0.30
Dewsbury MB	6	4	0.24
Halifax CB	35	4	0.75
Huddersfield CB	98	9	1.96
Keighley MB	8		0.39
Leeds CB	125	44	0.59
Morley MB	3		0.26
Ossett MB	3	2	0.45
Pontefract MB	4	3	0.48
Wakefield MB	5	2	0.19

Table 3
Conscientious Objectors[50]

Arrested	6,261
Work of National Importance (Pelham Committee)	3,964
Friends' Ambulance Unit (FAU)	1,200
Working directly with local tribunals	200
Non-Combatant Corps	3,300
Royal Army Medical Corp	100
Evaded the Act	175
Total	16,100

John W. Graham, *Conscription and Conscience: A History 1916-1919* (London, 1922)

Table 4
Huddersfield COs by Motivation[51]

Socialists	45	15 BSP, 1 Fabian Socialist, 7 ILP, 7 SSS (Socialist Sunday School) and 15 'Socialists'
Religious	44	1 Anglican, 18 Christadelphian, 1 Congregationalist, 1 Methodist 1 Primitive Methodist, 13 Quaker, 3 Wesleyan, 2 Roman Catholics 2 'Religious'
Other	10	1 Fellowship of Reconciliation, 7 No-Conscription Fellowship, 2 Union of Democratic Control, 1 Moral and Ethical
Not known	18	
TOTAL	117	

Conclusion

War changed progressive politics in Britain and may have contributed to the subsequent decline of the Liberal Party. However, Labour was just as divided as the Liberals on the issue of war, even though there were exceptional areas, such as Huddersfield, where there may have been a 'community of conscience' generally opposing war. What kept the Labour movement united was that the majority of the Labour movement, even the members of the ILP and the Bradford ILP, were pro-war and patriotic. Although the introduction of conscription in January 1916 changed attitudes towards war it did so more along the lines of the UDC demand for a negotiated peace and the various strands of labour opinion were bound together by the War Emergency: Workers' National Committee which unified them further through fighting to improve the conditions of working people by attacking profiteering, encouraging the 'conscription of riches' campaign *en route* to forming a vague policy on public ownership. The divided Labour movement was thus more fortunate in its wartime experience than the divided Liberal Party and enhanced its position in the progressive politics of Britain during the inter-war years. However, the successful outcome for Labour was often achieved at the cost of great personal anguish as the Rev. Roberts, a leading Bradford Labour activist, found when he changed his position from taking up the 'Fiery Cross' against militarism at the beginning of 1914 to one, shortly after the outbreak of war, of it being 'Better to die than to be Prussianised' or under the 'Prussian jackboot'. Attitudes towards war, in the Labour movement and Britain as a whole were refracted through religion, gender, racial, and social institutions and far more complex than ones of being pro-war and anti-war.

Notes

1. Arthur Marwick, *Britain in a Century of Total War* (London, 1968), p. 84.
2. Trevor Wilson, *The Decline of the Liberal Party* (London, 1966), p. 29.
3. Paul Ward, *Red Flag and Union Jack: Englishness, Patriotism and the British Left, 1881-1924* (Suffolk, 1998), chapter 7, pp. 119-141.
4. Robert Blatchford, *General von Sneak: A little study of war* (London, Hodder & Stoughton, 1918).
5. Chushichi Tsuzuki, *H. M. Hyndman and British Socialism* (Oxford, 1961), p. 243.

6. Cyril Pearce, *Comrades in Conscience: The story of an English community's opposition to the Great War* (London, Francis Boutle, originally published 2001 but revised and published in 2014), particularly look at p. 17 on the comments of Wilfrid Whiteley.

7. J. M. Winter, *Socialism and the Challenge of War: Ideas and Politics in Britain, 1912-1918* (London, 1974), particularly chapter 7, 'Sidney Webb and the War Emergency Committee', pp. 184-233; Ward, *Red Flag and Union Jack*, pp. 119-141; Royden Harrison, 'The War Emergency: Workers National Committee 1914-1920' in Asa Briggs and John Saville (eds) *Essays in Labour History 1886-1925* (London, 1971), pp. 211-59.

8. *Bradford Pioneer*, 9 January 1914.

9. G. Haupt, *Socialism and the Great War: The Collapse of the Second International* (London, 1972), particularly chapter 10, pp. 195-215.

10. Colin Cross, *Philip Snowden* (London, 1966), p, 128; Keith Laybourn, *Philip Snowden; A Biography* (Aldershot, Gower/Wildwood, 1988).

11. Bradford Trades and Labour Council, *Year Book*, 1912 (Bradford Trades Council, 1913), pp. 47-51, and supplementary information from the *Year Books* for 1913 (Bradford Trades Council, 1914) and 1914 (Bradford Trades Council, 1915).

12. Bradford and Trades Labour Council, Minutes, 7 November 1912, also quote by Fred Jowett in the report in the *Bradford Pioneer*, 7 August 1914 of his speech 2 August 1914.

13. *Bradford Pioneer*, 7 August 1914.

14. *Bradford Pioneer*, 21 May 1915.

15. *Bradford Weekly Telegraph*, 23 July 1915.

16. *Bradford Pioneer*, 25 February 1916.

17. *Bradford Pioneer*, 1 March 1918.

18. *Merthyr Pioneer*, 14 August 1914.

19. *Bradford Pioneer*, 20 December 1918.

20. *Bradford Pioneer*, 22 October 1915.

21. *Bradford Pioneer*, 23 December 1914.

22. Pearce, *Comrades in Conscience*, p.143. The long-established figures John W. Graham, *Conscription and Conscience: A History 1916-1919* (London, 1921) suggest that there may have been about 16,100 COs in Britain and that there were 59 COs in Bradford and 8 other in the Friends Ambulance Unit. Pearce, after gathering extensive information together, suggests that the total has to be revised upwards to between 20,662 and 23, 032 on his calculations based upon studies of undercounting in Huddersfield and other areas. Graham figures about 0.44 per thousand of those eligible for military conscription in Bradford were COs, although Pearce's adjustments would suggests that that may be at a minimum of 0.55 per thousand.

25

23. *Bradford Daily Telegraph*, 30 December 1918. Willie Leach later became MP for Bradford Central 1922-1924, 1929-1931, and 1935 to 1945.

24. Cited in F. Brockway, *Socialism over Sixty Years: The Life of Jowett of Bradford 1864-1944* (London, 1946), p. 152.

25. Republished from the *Merthyr Pioneer*, in the *Bradford Pioneer*, 21 April 1916.

26. *Bradford Pioneer*. 9 April 1915.

27. *Bradford Pioneer*, 14 August 1914.

28. *Bradford Pioneer,* 16 October 1914.

29. Kevin McPhillips, *Joseph Burgess (1853-1934) and the founding of the Independent Labour Party* (Lampeter, 2005), chapter 12, pp. 141-154.

30. Pearce, *Comrades in Conscience* (2001 version), p. 217.

31. His daughter Nora became Nora Feinburgh and had a son named Wilfred Feinburgh, who became a promising Labour MP before being killed in a motorbike accident.

32. *Bradford Pioneer*, 20 July 1917.

33. *Bradford Pioneer*, 27 July 1917.

34. *Bradford Pioneer*, 9 November 1917.

35. *Bradford Pioneer*, 9 November 1917.

36. Trevor Wilson, *The Myriad Faces of War* (Cambridge, 1986), p. 349.

37. Max Hastings, *Catastrophe: Europe Goes to War 1914* (London, 2013), amongst his many publications.

38. Bradford Trades and Labour Council (BTLC), Minutes, 17 June 1915.

39. BTLC, Minutes, and circular, 10 December 1915.

40. BTLC, Minutes, 29 November 1917.

41. Mary Ashraf, *Bradford Trades Council 1872-1972* (Bradford, 1972), p.94.

42. David Raw, *Bradford Pals: The Comprehensive History of the 16th, 18th and 20th (Service) Battalion of the Prince of Wales Own West Yorkshire Regiment 1914-1918* (Barnsley, 2006).

43. David Taylor, *Memory, Narrative and the Great War: Rifleman Patrick McGill and the Construction of Wartime Experience* (Liverpool, 2013); Paul Ward, 'Women of Britain say go: women's patriotism in the First World War, *Twentieth Century British History*, 12 (1), 23-48.

44. The Bradford Branch of the War Emergency: Workers' National Committee are to be found in the Bradford branch of the West Yorkshire Archives, the Central Library, Bradford.

45. Winter, *Socialism and the Challenge of War* , chapter 7.

46. Much of this section is based upon Pearce, *Comrades in Conscience* (mainly the 2014 edition) and Cyril Pearce, 'Shaping a Radical Community - Labour in West Yorkshire 1906 to 1918', in *Sons and Daughters*

of Labour: A history and recollection of the Labour Party within the historical boundaries of the West Riding of Yorkshire, edited by B. Evans, G. Haigh, J. Lancaster and K. Laybourn (Huddersfield, 2007).

47. Pearce, *Comrades in Conscience.*

48. Pearce, 'Shaping a Radical Community', p. 24.

49. Pearce, 'Shaping a Radical Community', p. 23.

50. John W. Graham, *Conscription and Conscience: A History 1916-1919* (London, 1922)

51. Pearce, *Comrades in Conscience.*

Radical Opposition to the First World War

Duncan Bowie

On the declaration of war against Germany, four members of Asquith's Cabinet offered their resignations – John Burns, John Morley, John Simon and Lord Beaumont. They were joined by one junior Minister, Charles Trevelyan. These resignations demonstrate that the Liberal Government was far from united – and there is a case that in fact there was a majority of Cabinet members opposed to joining the European war and that the British entry into the war was driven not so much by the German invasion of Belgium, but by the Foreign Secretary Sir Edward Grey's secret commitments to France and Russia and by the First Lord of the Admiralty, Winston Churchill's premature mobilisation of the fleet. The British entry into the war was far from inevitable. The purpose of this article is to trace the origins of the Liberal opposition to engaging in the carnage.

The Anti-War Traditions

Within the Liberal party there was a strong anti-war tradition. In fact there were a number of different traditions. Firstly, there was the free trade and anti-war tradition of the Manchester School, represented by Richard Cobden – the perspective that war interrupted free trade and that trade between nations was the way to avoid a European war but also that trade rather than imperial conquest was the most effective way of extending civilisation to what were seen as the least civilised parts of the world. This perspective was adopted by Gladstone both as Prime Minister (despite his reluctant sanction of a number of imperial adventures) and in opposition (for example in the Bulgarian atrocities campaign of 1876) – a tradition inherited by John Morley, Irish Secretary, Gladstone's biographer and the elder statesman in Asquith's 1914 Cabinet, and by leading Liberal intellectuals such as James Bryce.

Thirdly, there was the positivist tradition - in effect a belief that both national and world progress depended on cooperation between national states rather than aggressive imperial competition - this perspective was best demonstrated in Richard Congreve's essays on International Policy and the Anti-aggression League established by the positivist and active Liberal, Frederick Harrison, to argue against the wars in the Sudan and Afghanistan in the 1880s.

There was then the Quaker pacifist tradition, exemplified by the Peace Society led by the Welsh radical MP Henry Richards, but also represented by John Bright, who resigned from Gladstone's government in 1882 in protest against the naval bombardment of Alexandria in Egypt. There was an even earlier Liberal tradition of world federation and international governance originating with Jeremy Bentham in the 1820s which influenced radical and socialist thinkers throughout the 19th century, notably the Owenites, and especially the radicals in the years before the First World War.

There was also a strong internationalist tradition within working class Liberalism. This can be traced back to the Chartist William Lovett, who adopted Bentham's arguments for international government, the international solidarity movements of late Chartists such as George Julian Harney and William Linton, which with the increasing propaganda efforts of European republicans such as Mazzini and Kossuth, generated significant support among radical Liberal MPs such as Joseph Cowen of Newcastle and Peter Taylor of Leicester.

Important but less studied by historians of the Labour and radical movements (with the notable exception of Paul Laity) is the active engagement in international peace movements of a number of London based trade unionists. Both the Reform League of 1865 and the International Working Men's Association (or First International) of 1864, actually emerged from international solidarity movements established by London radicals and trade unionists, which focused on solidarity with Polish republicans and French trade unionists. A number of London trade unionists had been active supporters of the North in the American Civil War. In 1870, while Marx was writing his polemics on the French civil war and the Commune, William Randal Cremer together with other London trade unionists, George Odger, Ben Lucraft and Thomas Mottershead, established a Workmen's Peace Committee, with Edmond Beales of the Reform League as its chairman.

As is well known, Cremer and other London trade unionists including Mottershead, Robert Applegarth and George Howell withdrew from the First International, in the case of Odger and Lucraft, who had both played leading roles within the organisation, when Marx added their signatures to his Civil War in France pamphlet supporting the Paris Commune without asking for their agreement. Cremer switched his attention from international trade union solidarity to the international peace movement and established the Arbitration and Peace Association. He became the Liberal MP for

Haggerston and Shoreditch in 1885 and was awarded the Nobel Peace Prize in 1903. He was also co-founder of the Inter-Parliamentary Union and the International Arbitration League.

A number of other working class Liberal MPs known to posterity as the 'Lib-Labs' were also active in the international peace movement, including the Northumbrian miner, Thomas Burt, the agricultural workers' leader, Joseph Arch, Frederick Maddison, compositor, TUC president and MP for Sheffield Brightside, James Rowlands, watchmaker and MP for East Finsbury and then for Dartford, Henry Broadhurst, stonemason, TUC secretary, MP for Stoke and Home Office under secretary under Gladstone in 1885 and Ben Pickard, miner and MP for Normanton in Yorkshire.

Opposition to the Boer War

The Boer War of 1899-1902 witnessed growing opposition to imperialist ventures within the leadership of the Liberal party. While Liberal imperialists such as Prime Minister Lord Roseberry, Grey and Asquith supported intervention, critics of the war included Henry Campbell Bannerman, who was to become Prime Minister in 1906, James Bryce, Henry Labouchere, Leonard Courtney, John Morley and William Harcourt, who had been Home Secretary in Gladstone's last government. Campbell Bannerman attacked 'methods of barbarism' while Labouchere chaired 'Stop the War' rallies. Cremer's International Arbitration League in 1899 also included almost all of the Lib-Lab MPs – Arch, Broadhurst, Maddison, Pickard, and Burt, together with Charles Fenwick, Will Steadman and John Wilson.

By the mid-1900s, with Grey pursuing an imperialist foreign policy first under Campbell Bannerman and then under Asquith, the anti–imperialists were joined by a group of radical journalists – G H Perris, Henry Nevinson, H N Brailsford, W C Stead, Wilfrid Scawen Blunt, and Norman Angell, author of The Great Illusion, together with the journalist and economist, J A Hobson, who had been a critic of the Boer War and of broader imperialist policies and in fact the source of much of Lenin's thinking on the subject.

Given this historical background, it is therefore not surprising that in the late summer of 1914 there was strong the opposition to engaging in a European war both within Asquith's Liberal government and within the wider Liberal party. Douglas Newton, in his recent book, *The Darkest Days: the Truth behind Britain's Rush to War*, demonstrates that there was a majority within the Cabinet in favour of some form of neutralism and avoiding a commitment to support France or Russia. He also demonstrates that Britain was committed to war before the Germans invaded Belgium, though this invasion provided a useful retrospective justification. He also demonstrates that there was no treaty obligation for Britain to support France, though the Foreign Secretary, Grey, thought there was a moral obligation and considered that Britain was honour bound to intervene to support its Entente ally. In fact he threatened to resign if Britain remained neutral, and Asquith would have resigned with him. It was the possibility of the government falling and being replaced by a Liberal imperialist/Tory war coalition that kept some of the more neutralist ministers within the government.

Churchill pre-empts the Cabinet

It was actually Winston Churchill as Lord of the Admiralty who was to pre-empt Cabinet decisions by ordering the mobilisation of the navy, which encouraged both Russia and France to adopt a more aggressive position. *The Times* led a pro-war campaign, and Churchill certainly encouraged the Tory leadership of Andrew Bonar Law and Austen Chamberlain to adopt a pro-intervention position. It is Newton's study of the Liberal neutralists which is perhaps most interesting. John Burns, often criticised by socialist historians, was the strongest opponent of intervention and resigned first, to be followed by John Morley. John Simon, the solicitor general and future Liberal leader and Lord Beauchamp, Liberal leader in the Lords, also resigned, but were persuaded to keep their resignations secret and to rejoin the Cabinet once war was actually declared. Beauchamp was to chair the Privy Council meeting with the King which signed the declaration of war. Interestingly, neither Parliament nor Cabinet formally debated the declaration of war. Some 16 backbench radical MPs managed to speak on an adjournment debate just before the declaration, but no vote was taken, and the Liberal leadership, including the Cabinet dissidents, absented itself from the debate.

In the last few days before the war, the radicals established a British Neutrality Committee. This was led by Arthur Ponsonby who established a Liberal Foreign Affairs Group, and Charles Trevelyan, who resigned his junior ministerial role as parliamentary secretary to the Board of Education, with the Fabian Graham Wallas. Trevelyan had previously published a pamphlet for the National League of Young Liberals on Democracy and Compulsory Service which opposed conscription.

The foreign policy dissident, Norman Angell, established his own British Neutrality League. On the eve of the declaration of war, on Sunday 2nd August, a mass anti-war rally of 20,000 people was held in Trafalgar Square, called by the British Section of the Second International, whose leaders had just returned from a crisis meeting in Brussels. Keir Hardie was among the speakers, together with Arthur Henderson, Ben Tillett and Robert Smillie and the leaders of the labour women's movement, who had been active in opposing the rush to war - Charlotte Despard (General French's sister), Margaret Bondfield, Mary MacArthur and Marion Phillips.

A number of radical Liberals favoured neutralism, but did not publicly oppose Grey and Asquith and stayed in the Cabinet. The role of Lulu Harcourt, chief whip and son of Sir William Harcourt, is critical here. Radicals such as Reginald McKenna, the Quaker Joseph Pease (who was actually president of the Peace Society) and Herbert Samuel also supported Asquith and Grey and stayed within the government. Charles Masterman, radical on domestic issues, was a Liberal imperialist when it came to foreign policy. So an administration with a neutralist majority was forced to adopt an interventionist policy under pressure from Grey, Churchill and to a lesser extent Asquith, combined with the 'force of events'.

The British government, despite the large number of neutralists within it, actually contributed to the outbreak of the continental war. This was not inevitable. Grey rejected a number of opportunities for negotiation and on a number of occasions clearly misled the Cabinet and Parliament. Churchill could not wait to get the war started. He kept arguing that a quick naval war would cost very little to the British taxpayers.

Union for the Democratic Control of Foreign Policy (UDC)

With their attempt to keep Britain neutral unsuccessful, Trevelyan and Ponsonby, together with Norman Angell and Ramsay MacDonald, considering that it was the secret commitments pursued by Grey, that had dragged Britain into the war, established a new organisation – the Union for the Democratic Control of Foreign Policy, to be known as the UDC. Appointing the anti-colonialist, Edmund Morel, as secretary, the UDC was active throughout the war and in the interwar period, campaigning against secret treaties and for open government. In the early years of the war, the UDC published pamphlets by Norman Angell, Bertrand Russell, Brailsford and Ponsonby. The latter published in 1915 *Democracy and Diplomacy – A Plea for Popular Control of Foreign Policy*, which put forward the idea of a foreign affairs committee in Parliament. In 1918, the UDC published the text of the secret treaties with Russia, Italy, France and Japan relating to the breakup of the Ottoman Empire, the division of Persia, the transfer of Istria from the Austro-Hungarian Empire to Italy and the west bank of the Rhine. The UDC also acted as a forum for radical Liberals to co-operate with anti-war socialists, and a route by which Trevelyan, Morel and Ponsonby among others, transferred their allegiance from the Liberal party to the Labour party.

Some of the radicals later wrote their own justifications for their actions. Morley's 1914 Memorandum on Resignation was not published until 1928 after his death. Morley had in the pre-war years supported Anglo-German understanding as a bulwark against Russian expansionism. He was highly critical of what he saw as 'Russian barbarism' and did not consider Russian dominance of Europe as good for Western civilisation. He wrote that 'to bind ourselves to France is at the same time to bind ourselves to Russia'. He considered Russia not Germany as the real aggressor and did not consider German aggression against Belgium as a justification for the British declaration of war on Germany. He considered that 'the atmosphere of war cannot be friendly to order in a democratic system'. Morley refused to follow Simon and Beauchamp in rejoining the Cabinet - he considered himself as a notorious 'peace man' and 'Little Englander'.

In contrast, Burns never publicly recorded the reasons for his resignation, though he recorded his views in his diary. He was an isolationist – believing that Britain should not get involved in the continental war. He was not a pacifist – in fact he had an interest in military matters, especially regimental history. He was in 1906 a member of Haldane's Cabinet committee on army reform and attended military manoeuvres on Salisbury Plain. In 1915 he commented that his position was 'splendid isolation, no balance of power, no incorporation in the continental system'. He had also been active in Cremer's International Arbitration League, and at one dinner gave a toast to Anglo-German friendship. The main reason for his resignation was his shock to discover Grey's secret diplomacy. He was also disgusted with the warmongering of much of the press. Once taken, his decision was final.

The Country was Misled

Trevelyan gave an explanation for his resignation in his memoir *From Liberalism to Labour*, published in 1921. Like Burns, he was opposed to Grey's secret treaties and the commitments given to France. When Asquith supported Grey, while denying that Britain had any legal commitments, he felt there was no alternative but to resign. In his memoir he wrote: 'On August 3 1914 it was proved that the information given to Parliament on the most vital question in a hundred years was incorrect, I therefore resigned my subordinate position in the Liberal government which had misled the county.' He added that 'the war was settled by the Cabinet before Parliament was consulted. Parliament had no power of choice left.'

Other radicals were also to put their position on the record. Robert Reid, Earl Loreburn, who had been Lord Chancellor between 1905 and 1912, published in 1919 a critique of Grey's foreign policy in *How the War Came*. The first detailed narrative of the diplomatic manoeuvres which led to the war was actually published in 1915 in New York by the former Liberal MP and playwright, Francis Neilson in *How Diplomats Make War*. Neilson argued that the arms build-up and secret diplomacy of Grey contributed to the outbreak of war. The book was written within six weeks of his resignation from Parliament and his 'flight' to America.

The UDC was in fact to continue in existence until 1966 – in the period after the Second World War it published pamphlets on colonialism in Nyasaland and Northern Rhodesia, a pamphlet on the Suez crisis by the left-wing Labour MP Frank Allaun and on the Russian intervention in Hungary in 1956 by historian Basil Davidson. One of its last pamphlets was in fact a critique of misgovernment in the Seychelles by a Peckham vicar, Charles Roach. Ponsonby was to become under-secretary of foreign affairs in Macdonald's first government in 1924 – Macdonald acted as his own Foreign Minister.

Ponsonby introduced a new constitutional convention: that any proposed treaty should be put to Parliament 21 days before ratification. This reflected his experience of 1914, when there was no parliamentary vote, and where the declaration was made by the king in Privy Council. The convention was not followed when Tony Blair's government decided to invade Iraq. The Ponsonby rule was actually incorporated in British statute on 11 November 2010 under Part 2 of the Constitutional Reform and Governance Act – 96 years after the start of the First World War.

This is an edited version of the lecture given at Conway Hall, 21 October 2014.

From Slaughter to Mutiny
Ian Birchall

> General, your tank is a powerful vehicle
> It smashes down forests and crushes a hundred men.
> But it has one defect:
> It needs a driver.
>
> General, your bomber is powerful.
> It flies faster than a storm and carries more than an elephant.
> But it has one defect:
> It needs a mechanic.
>
> General, man is very useful.
> He can fly and he can kill.
> But he has one defect:
> He can think.
>
> *Bertolt Brecht*[1]

In 1914 millions of men across Europe went to war. Tory Minister Michael Gove assures us that these men were 'not dupes',[2] and who are we to disagree? In fact it's clear that many went to war because they genuinely believed in the defence of their native country – and many more went because they felt it was their duty or were pressured in various ways.

Often their initial motivations did not survive the experience of trench warfare; what they had expected would be a short war became both unimaginably horrific and apparently everlasting. Some deserted, others resorted to self-mutilation (for which, in the French army, the punishment was to be tied up and thrown into No Man's Land.)[3] In some areas of the front soldiers engaged in what Tony Ashworth has described as the 'live and let live system',[4] whereby a tacit agreement between rank-and-file soldiers was made to minimise casualties. Despite this, casualties continued at a horrific rate.

By 1917 discontent was growing, and the years 1917 to 1919 were marked by waves of strikes and mutinies right across Europe – and beyond.[5] I am here just going to look at three instances – the French army mutinies of 1917, the German naval mutinies of November 1918 and the French naval mutinies in the Black Sea in 1919. Mutiny is a fateful decision for soldiers. Strikers can walk out and, if they fail to win, they go back to work. Failed mutineers face execution or long jail sentences. But faced with a high mortality rate, generals who were quite happy to squander their soldiers' lives with foolish attacks and a war which seemed to be continuing interminably, many soldiers came to feel that they had nothing to lose by mutiny.

In May and June 1917 there were widespread mutinies in the French army, reaching a peak around 2 June. It is very difficult to calculate exactly how many men were involved – one recent estimate puts the figure at between thirty and eighty thousand mutineers,[6] out of a total army strength of a little under two million. Obviously many more who did not actively mutiny were touched by the general mood of discontent that affected a large part of the army.

The mutinies were often simple – apparently spontaneous – refusals to obey orders. A couple of incidents are recorded as follows:

Thus one battalion was due to make its way to the trenches. The men had formed up without incident. But when the signal from the battalion leader sounded, nobody moved. The companies remained lined up behind stacks of rifles and kit bags.

There were a few seconds of anguished expectancy ... The whistle was blown a second time, and again there was no movement. The situation was suddenly obvious.

The whole troop remained a state of immobility which might seem concerted, in order, but refusing to obey.

In another incident:

The battalion was stationed in a mushroom farm with the divisional headquarters. When they were told to pick up their kit bags, nobody moved, the candles went out and it was pitch dark. Every time an officer lit a candle, it was immediately put out. It was impossible to assemble the troops. When orders were given, the men replied with sneers and insults. The divisional officers tried to intervene and exhort the men to do their duty, but they were shouted down.[7]

Among those who mutinied were many of the Russian soldiers who had been sent to France to fight on the Western Front. They had heard news of the fall of the Tsar and refused to fight. The authorities were very keen to isolate them from French soldiers so that revolutionary ideas would not spread. Eventually they were taken away and shelled into submission. Many of the survivors who remained intransigent were then deported to Algeria.[8]

Also involved were some of the troops brought from the French colonies to assist with the war. These were treated particularly badly.

Of 157,000 black African troops brought to Europe some 30,000 were killed, a very high proportion. Some Senegalese troops literally died of cold, as the French army provided no alternative to the tropical clothing they had worn at home.[9] When a mutiny broke out among Senegalese troops in August 1917, the authorities made some concessions, being afraid that too heavy repression might have a disastrous impact on other Senegalese, Madagascan and Indochinese troops.[10]

Obviously the initiative in the mutinies was often taken by individuals, some of whom were probably politically motivated, or may have been influenced by the extensive anti-militarist propaganda carried out by the trade unions in pre-1914 France. But there was no central political leadership or coordination to organise the movement. As a result it was often extremely volatile. Rumours and false information undoubtedly played a significant part.

Anti-war literature, whether anarchist, socialist or syndicalist, circulated widely among troops at the front, and undoubtedly contributed to the degree of dissatisfaction, and encouraged soldiers to stand up for their rights.[11]

One demand that arose in a number of places was the idea of a march on Paris. Clearly this represented the recognition of the need for a political solution, a wish to force the government to bring the war to an end. But without any political leadership it was very unclear how this could be achieved. In fact the authorities had little difficulty in sealing off the railway stations and suspending the train service to Paris.[12]

What remains a matter of dispute among historians is to what extent the mutinies were "political". Were the soldiers simply in revolt against poor conditions and a military strategy which seemed wasteful of human life, or were they committed to bringing the war to an end?[13]

The truth seems to lie somewhere in the middle. Those involved in the mutinies had a variety of motives; as an eyewitness to one mutiny reported: 'Some wanted peace, some wanted to go on leave, and others were singing the *Internationale*.'[14] But what is clear is that consciousness was very fluid. Soldiers who had decided to reject military discipline and to refuse to do as their officers told them were moving into uncharted waters. Even if their initial motivation derived from specific discontents about conditions, they were moving into a new situation where they were open to new ideas; the old certainties that had held their world together were collapsing. Those who survived the next year and a half of fighting would return to civilian life profoundly radicalised; many would become involved in the *Clarté* movement[15] or would help to found the French Communist Party.

The soldiers rapidly improvised forms of organisation – for example by the use of flying pickets to try and spread the action to other sections of the army.[16] But without any political coordination it was too little, too late. Moreover, there was the problem of unity between the soldiers and industrial workers. Troops in the trenches often felt initial hostility when they heard of strikes behind the lines, feeling that civilians were having a much easier time of it than they were. So even when, as in France in the summer of 1917, strikes in the munitions factories coincided with mutinies in the trenches, it was not possible to bring the two together in a way which could have posed a real revolutionary challenge to the regime.

So the authorities, headed by General Pétain, were able to regain the upper hand. Repression was severe; there were 629 death sentences,[17] though most were commuted; there were between 26 and 57 executions (it is difficult to disentangle which were directly linked to the mutinies and which were for other offences).[18] There was also an attempt to weed out 'trouble-makers' and send them to Africa or Indochina. Many were also sentenced to imprisonment; most of these were amnestied in 1921 or 1925, but a few stayed in jail till 1933.[19]

But it was not a total defeat. Pétain and the government recognised that the mutinies had shown a real threat of the break-down of discipline; they responded with both stick and some rather small carrots.

All soldiers were to be guaranteed seven days leave every four months, with additional rest periods away from the front line. The quality of food was to be improved, with kitchens as near as possible to the trenches.[20] But if Pétain abandoned the strategy of offensive *à outrance*, which had led to particularly heavy casualties, life in the trenches did not change much.[21]

The French mutinies formed part of an international conjuncture. Working-class support for the war, which had undoubtedly been very real in 1914, was beginning to wear dangerously thin. In Italy there were massive strikes, building up to the near-insurrectionary struggles in Turin in 1917. In September 1917 the biggest mutiny in the British army, at Étaples, took place.[22] And in Russia the collapse of army discipline was part of the situation that made the two revolutions possible. Between February and October 1917 there were some two million desertions – by the end of the year one deserter for every three men in the field.[23]

There were also mutinies in the German Navy in the summer of 1917, but they were only a prelude to the much more serious events in the last months of 1918. The conditions of sailors were very different from those of soldiers. Soldiers in trench warfare were constantly on the move and suffered an appalling casualty rate. Although political literature and political ideas circulated widely, the possibility of developing any kind of political organisation was very limited.

A large ship was a different matter. Here several hundred men lived together in a confined space; unless the ship was sunk there were few casualties; in fact the German Navy saw relatively little combat, and the ships were kept in port where sailors could maintain contact with the labour movement on shore. Modern ships required skilled workers, and many seamen were technicians and skilled artisans who often had some experience of the trade-union movement. In short, there was a lot in common between a ship and a factory.[24]

Moreover, the class divisions on a ship were extremely visible. The officers enjoyed enormous privileges in terms of food, accommodation and so on, and they treated the common sailors with contempt. On one ship the seamen were required to row their officers ashore so that they could visit the local brothels, and then wait all night in the cold until the officers were ready to return to the ship.[25] As a result there was enormous festering discontent which eventually exploded.

By August 1918 it was clear that Germany could not win the war; a new mildly liberal government was formed to prepare for the inevitable looming defeat. But the heads of the navy did not accept this situation; they wanted to go down fighting – in Daniel Horn's words they wanted to 'order the High Seas Fleet out on a desperate and heroic but completely hopeless and illegal suicide mission against the British'.[26] As rumours of this began to spread, the sailors became implacably opposed to any attempt to sacrifice their lives for the ambitions of the hated officer class.

Thus a contemporary report of events on the Thüringen, which had been the model ship of the fleet tells us:

> The crew simply locked up the petty officers and refused to weigh anchor. The men told the captain that would only fight against the

39

English if their fleet appeared in German waters. They no longer wanted to risk their lives uselessly.[27]

Very rapidly radical demands were raised: the Sailors' Council of the First Torpedo Division produced a set of demands that included abdication of the royal family; release of political prisoners; universal suffrage for men and women; and immediate peace.[28] When the heads of the navy agreed to negotiate on some of the men's demands, they took this as a sign that they had won:

> The enlisted men of Kiel rose up in jubilation and took over the town. Ten thousand of them staged an impromptu parade in which they marched to the jails and freed all political prisoners.[29]

As Daniel Horn describes, the revolutionary movement now spread very rapidly and moved beyond the navy and the coastal towns:

> As early as November 4, individual sailors and groups of sailors had begun streaming out of Kiel by truck, train, and ship, fomenting revolution wherever they went. Illustrative of this process are actions of the Third Squadron of the High Seas Fleet. On November 5 that unit, flying the red flag of revolution, had anchored at Travemünde and landed five hundred men who marched off towards Lübeck. Without their firing a shot, the entire town with its garrison had surrendered and gone over to the revolution.[30]

Within a couple of days:

> on November 7 .... a band of sailors waving red flags arrived by train in Cologne. Within a few hours they subverted a garrison of forty-five thousand men, opened all the jails, and assumed power through a sailors' council.[31]

Within a matter of days the sailors had evolved from making demands that related specifically to their life on board ship – such as equal rations for officers and enlisted men and freedom not to salute officers when off duty[32] – to challenging the whole social and economic system. As with the French mutinies, ideas were in a state of flux; the sailors were setting out to change things, and in the process they were changing themselves.

A fascinating insight into how people and their ideas change is provided by the diary of seaman Richard Stumpf. Stumpf served as an ordinary seaman throughout the war; he was a devout Catholic and generally nationalistic and conservative in his attitudes; yet he bitterly resented the bullying arrogance of the officers. He recorded his experience of the mutinies, and the way he and his fellow-sailors were beginning to realise their power:

What has happened to the almighty power of the proud captains and staff engineers? Now, at last, after many years, the suppressed stokers and sailors realize that nothing, no, nothing, can be accomplished without them. Can this be possible? After having lived for such a long, long time under this iron discipline, this corpse-like obedience, it appears hardly possible.

He was becoming increasingly aware of the contradiction between his own conservatism and his hatred and resentment of the officer class:

Long years of accumulated injustice have been transformed into a dangerously explosive force which now erupts with great power all around. My God – why did we have to have such criminal, conscienceless officers? It was they who deprived us of all our love for the fatherland, our joy in our German existence, and our pride for our incomparable institutions. Even now my blood boils with anger whenever I think of the many injustices I suffered in the navy.... Now, however, it feels wonderful to demonstrate our power, to ignore orders and to assert ourselves.

And he noted, almost in surprise:

Within the past two days an unbelievable change has taken place within me. [I have been converted] from a monarchist into a devout republican.[33]

On 9 November Germany itself was converted into a republic; two days later the war came to an end. The naval mutinies had led to a process which overthrew the monarchy. For the next five years Germany appeared to be on the very brink of revolution. If it had succeeded Hitler's name would never have been known and 'socialism in one country' would have been a meaningless notion. The reasons why this did not happen are outside the scope of this paper.[34]

But already western leaders had a fresh target – they wanted to overthrow the Bolshevik regime in Russia, which offered workers in the west a model of an alternative to the society that had produced so much death and destruction. On 30 October 1918 an armistice was signed with Turkey, opening up the Dardanelles to the Allies. On 16 November Allied ships entered the Black Sea. A large number of French warships were sent to the Black Sea and the ports of Odessa, in the Ukraine, and Sebastopol, in the Crimea, were occupied by French troops.

But there was now a widespread feeling among the rank and file that they had done the job they joined up for, and that they should go home. Among troops sent to the Ukraine was the 58th infantry regiment, originating from Avignon, which had a revolutionary action committee. Some of these were soldiers who had mutinied on the French front in 1917 and had been deported to the Eastern army. In early February, it was the first regiment to refuse to fight against the Bolsheviks. The regiment was disarmed, and then sent to Morocco, where its men were drafted into disciplinary companies. The Bolsheviks realised that their best hope was to try and win support from the soldiers and sailors being sent to attack them, men who were war-weary and potentially sympathetic to the Bolshevik cause.

Necessarily this lecture has been mainly about men; but here I want to mention a remarkable woman who played a significant rôle in the process. Jeanne Labourbe was born into a peasant family in Burgundy in 1877, she was a shepherdess in her early years, but at the age of eighteen she went to work in Russia for a Polish family as maid and governess. In 1903 she became politically active for the first time. She knew Rosa Luxemburg and helped to smuggle people and correspondence across frontiers. At the time of the 1905 Revolution she joined the Bolshevik Party, being the first French member of that organisation. At the time of the October Revolution she was working as a teacher in Russia. In February the French Communist group in Russia agreed that she should immediately go to Odessa with a small group of supporters. Leaflets distributed by Odessa Communists explained to the French soldiers what Bolshevism was:

> You have been told about Bolshevism, and the bourgeois press has made a huge fuss about it, claiming that it is the establishment of arbitrary rule, that the Bolsheviks are thieves and criminals.
>
> Comrades, you must know the truth. A Bolshevik is an individual fighting for the immediate achievement of a socialist society. Bolshevism is socialist society in practice.
>
> It is the establishment of the power of workers and peasants, of those who have always been the tools of the rich and powerful, of those who have worked unceasingly and without reward in workshops, mills, factories, and in the fields, who have bled for the others in great battles. Bolshevism is the rule of workers' and peasants' councils (soviets), established in every town and village, and which control all countries. These councils are the only democratic form which can finally enable the proletarian class to rule for itself. That is what Bolshevism is.

Labourbe wrote articles and leaflets addressed to French troops. But she also took on the more risky, but absolutely necessary task of making direct contact with French troops. Members of her group talked to soldiers in the streets and cafés of the town. News spread through the barracks that there was a Frenchwoman in Odessa. She talked freely to French soldiers, addressing them as 'my children'. When she argued that the Bolsheviks were developing the revolutionary traditions of 1793 and the Commune, she got a rapid and sympathetic response from the young men. The French-language newspaper *Le Communiste* published letters from soldiers and sailors showing the development of an oppositional mood.

Clearly the French authorities could not allow this to continue. On 2 March a group of French and White Russian officers arrested Labourbe and a number of her comrades following betrayal by a provocateur. After interrogation six women were taken by car to a cemetery and there they were shot. Some of the women were raped and the bodies were viciously disfigured.

But the French authorities had to admit defeat. Just one month later it was decided that the troops were not reliable enough to hold Odessa, and the French withdrew. A pro-Bolshevik regime was re-established in the city. A hundred thousand people attended Labourbe's funeral.

Mutiny now spread to the French warships in the Black Sea. As in the German navy, warships had much in common with factories, and there was a high level of politicisation. On most of the French warships action committees had been formed, often instigated by sailors or petty officers who were engineers; engineers were often more revolutionary because of the similarity between their work and that of a factory worker.

One of the Socialist Party deputies, Pierre Brizon, who had attended the anti-war conference at Kienthal in 1916, edited the paper *La Vague* (The Wave) which had a circulation of 300,000. It had an enormous influence in the army and navy, where it was often passed around hundreds of readers. Each issue had a column of correspondence from soldiers and sailors. Cuttings from it reached soldiers, inserted inside reactionary papers. Or else the sailors took out a subscription to the paper, and if it arrived on board, even if it was confiscated by the officer in charge of censorship, the sailors had it returned to them surreptitiously by the officer's orderly.

There were a number of political activists on the ships, for example chief engineer André Marty, who had a long political past; he had been a professional seaman before 1914, involved with the socialist paper *Cri du marin*; since 1917 he had been in close contact with the revolutionary syndicalists and anti-war socialists from Paris.

Marty used to give technical instruction to the mechanics and stokers, but he took the opportunity to make political propaganda; he always began his lectures by saying that the working class would soon have to take over the running of society, and that therefore young workers should be prepared technically for the task. He also circulated copies of newspapers received by the ship's officers; although these were reactionary, they reported strikes and revolutionary events in Germany, Austria and Hungary, and helped to make the sailors aware of the world situation.[35]

A participant account describes how events developed:

On 16 April, the battleship France arrived at Sebastopol from Odessa. The landing party went ashore.

It was their job to block the advance of the Red Army which was approaching Sebastopol. On 17 April the ship's bugles called them to battle stations.

A substantial number of the engineers went on deck and refused to work as a sign of protest. Under threats from the NCOs, some sailors went down to the machines with a bad grace. The die-hards, who refused to obey, were arrested and locked up in the ship's cells.

It was then that the sailors realised that a peaceful demonstration had no chance of success. And they decided to take clearly revolutionary action.

The opportunity came some days later. The officer in command had decided that the loading of coal would take place on 20 April, which was Easter Sunday. It was a laborious task, and so there was great discontent.

The word went round: 'Those who don't want to carry coal, assemble on the forecastle, after piping to quarters in the evening.'

Lagaillarde, who had been appointed to give a lead to the meeting, first of all sang love songs, then the Odessa Song (a French revolutionary song, composed by unknown soldiers), then the *Internationale*. Almost all the crew turned up, with 600 men taking up the chorus. The officers were going crazy; they gathered on the quarter deck, and took up arms. The neighbouring Jean-Bart was joining in. In turn the sailors rushed to the stern where the infantry arms were stored, shouting 'Guns!' They went down to the prison cells and opened them up. Thus among others they released Virgile Vuillemin, a sailor-engineer aged twenty, who had been in solitary confinement and who was to take the lead of the mutiny. Vuillemin was elected at the same time as two other comrades.

The delegates presented their demands to the deputy commanding officer:

An end to the war against Russia;
Immediate return to France;
Less rigorous discipline;
Improved food;
Leave for the crew.

Then they went in a steam-launch to the battleship Jean-Bart and stated their demands: 'To Toulon! No more war against the Russians!' 'Rise up! Rise up! Revolution!' they shouted, shaking the hammocks.

Vice-Admiral Amet, commander of the fleet, arrived on board the France. Sailors and Admiral stood face to face. The Admiral's sermon was interrupted by shouts of 'Take him away! Kill him!' When he claimed that the Bolsheviks were bandits, a mutineer shouted at him: 'You're the biggest bandit.' The demonstrators abandoned Amet there and went to the quarter deck singing the *Internationale* and the Odessa Song. The Admiral, furious, left the ship shouting threats.

Amet had no more luck on the Jean-Bart. Almost all his musicians were playing the revolutionary anthem accompanied by the sailors singing in chorus. The officers of the ship then ordered hogsheads of wine to be brought up onto the deck in the hope of getting the crew drunk. But the mutineers placed a picket around the receptacles. Nobody touched them.

The next day, 20 April, Easter Sunday, almost all the sailors of the France and the Jean-Bart, instead of saluting the tricolour flag raised aft, stood facing the bow and sang the *Internationale*, while the red flag was raised on the bowsprit mast on both boats simultaneously.

A lieutenant-commander, shaking his fist at the red flag, shouted: 'You don't know what that rag stands for, it means civil war!' Two hundred sailors lined up three deep in front of the revolutionary standard. The Vice-Admiral came on board. When he approached the first row of men protecting the red flag, the sailors warned him that if he took one more step forward, they would throw him in the sea. There were shouts of: 'Kill him! Throw him in the water!'

The Admiral then gave the crews permission to go ashore. But it was a planned ambush. A group of sailors formed a procession singing the Internationale through the streets of Sebastopol, and received a warm welcome from the population. In front of the town hall the president of the Bolshevik revolutionary committee greeted the demonstrators. But a lieutenant-commander tried to grab the red flag and got a couple of smacks in the face. In response, without warning, salvoes of bullets swept across the street: fire had been opened by Greek soldiers and the sub-lieutenant, accompanied by two petty officers from a section of the landing party from the Jean-Bart, while for their part, the men were firing in the air. It was a massacre. There were a very large number of killed and wounded among the sailors and Soviet working-class population.[36]

But this setback did not prevent the mutinies from spreading. Thus on the battleship Justice which had anchored close to the other two,

the spark which set off the explosion was a simple task concerning potatoes. The sailors had only been given frozen or rotten potatoes to peel. There were lively protests. Vice-Admiral Amet, already very busy elsewhere, had just arrived on the battleship. He summoned the crew to assemble on the quarter deck. When he stated that it was necessary to 'bring down the Bolsheviks', the sailors could stand it no longer. They sang the *Internationale*. Then the superior officer made the ludicrous suggestion: 'Boys, sing the Madelon if you like. Not the *Internationale*.' Shouts burst out: 'Bandit! Throw him in the water!' He was jeered and potatoes were thrown at him as he left the ship shattered, while the red flag was raised.

A few days later, from 19 to 21 June, it was at Bizerta, then an important French war-port, that the crew of the battleship Voltaire rebelled, again as it was about to leave for the Black Sea. The stoker Alquier declared to the officer in command: 'The bourgeoisie can go to Russia if they want to. We have nothing to defend over there.'

Though the mutinies were suppressed eventually, they undoubtedly helped to relax the pressure on the Bolsheviks from the south, and make their contribution to enabling the Bolshevik state to survive. The mutineer most harshly treated was André Marty, who was sentenced to twenty years hard labour. A powerful propaganda campaign won an amnesty for the Black Sea mutineers in July 1922, but Marty was released only a year later. He went to be a leading member of the French Communist Party for thirty years before being expelled on bizarre charges in 1952.[37]

But despite the repression and victimisation, despite the subsequent setbacks, the mutinies should not be forgotten. They demonstrate that, in the last resort, war can only be fought if soldiers are willing to fight it, and that disobedience is the best way to bring fighting to an end.

This is an edited version of the lecture given at Conway Hall, 11 November 2014

Notes

1. https://www.goodreads.com/quotes/408232-general-your-tank-is-a-powerful-vehicle-it-smashes-down
2. *Daily Mail*, 2 January 2014 http://www.dailymail.co.uk/news/article-2532923/Michael-Gove-blasts-Blackadder-myths-First-World-War-spread-television-sit-coms-left-wing-academics.html
3. G Pedroncini, *Les Mutineries de 1917*, Paris, 1967, p. 25.
4. Tony Ashworth, *Trench Warfare 1914-1918: the live and let live system*, London, 1980.
5. See for example Sam Pollock, *Mutiny for the Cause*, London, 1969 on the 1920 mutiny by the Connaught Rangers in India.
6. A Loez, 14-18. *Les Refus de la guerre*, Paris, 2010, pp. 196-7, 235.
7. D Rolland, *La Grève des tranchées*, Paris, 2005, pp. 58, 299.
8. R Adam, 1917, *La Révolte des soldats russes en France*, Pantin, 2007.
9. See V G Kiernan, 'Colonial Africa and its Armies', in B Bond & I Roy (eds.), *War and Society* volume II (London, 1977), pp 20-39.
10. Rolland, *La Grève des tranchées*, pp. 301-2.
11. Pedroncini, *Les Mutineries de 1917*, p. 38 ; Rolland, *La Grève des tranchées*, p. 331.
12. Loez, 14-18, pp. 260-64.
13. See Pedroncini, *Les Mutineries de 1917* for the argument that the mutinies were 'non-political', and L V Smith, *Between Mutiny and Obedience*, Princeton NJ, 1994, for a critique of this position.
14. Loez, 14-18, p. 382.
15. See A Cuenot, *Clarté 1919-1924 : Tome I – Du pacifisme à l'internationalisme prolétarien*, Paris, 2011.
16. Loez, 14-18, pp. 304-5.
17. Pedroncini, *Les Mutineries de 1917*, p. 192.
18. Loez, 14-18, p. 513.
19. Rolland, *La Grève des tranchées,* pp. 388-92.
20. Pedroncini, *Les Mutineries de 1917*, pp. 235, 237, 242.
21. Smith, *Between Mutiny and Obedience,* p. 215.
22. See D Gill & G Dallas, *The Unknown Army*, London, 1985. See also http://londonsocialisthistorians.blogspot.co.uk/2014/05/ian-birchall-on-british-army-in-world.html
23. N N Golovine, *The Russian Army in the World War*, New Haven, 1931, pp. 260, 125, 197. (I am told these figures may be somewhat exaggerated.)
24. P Broué, *The German Revolution 1917-1923*, Leiden, 2005, p. 97; D Horn, *Mutiny on the High Seas*, London, 1973, p. 11.
25. Horn, *Mutiny on the High Seas*, p. 196.
26. Horn, *Mutiny on the High Seas*, p. 200.
27. *War, Mutiny and Revolution in the German Navy: The World war Diary of Seaman Richard Stumpf,* New Brunswick NJ, 1967, p. 419.

28. Horn, *Mutiny on the High Seas,* p. 246.
29. Horn, *Mutiny on the High Seas,* p. 247.
30. Horn, *Mutiny on the High Seas,* p. 259.
31. Horn, *Mutiny on the High Seas,* p. 265.
32. Horn, *Mutiny on the High Seas,* pp. 231-2.
33. *War, Mutiny and Revolution in the German Navy,* pp. 418-9, 420, 426.
34. For an analysis see Broué, The German Revolution.
35. André Marty, *La Révolte de la Mer Noire,* Paris, 1939, pp. 236, 238.
36. The quotations are from an article which appeared in Cahiers de Mai in 1969; it was written with the assistance of three participants in the mutinies, Marcel Monribot, Charles Tillon and Virgile Vuillemin. An English translation appeared in Revolutionary History Vol. 8, No. 2. Most of this section is based on this article.
37. See 'Pour lire la "Révolte de la Mer Noire André Marty révolution-naire'. Supplément à *Rouge* No. 74, Paris, 1970.

André Marty

'Down with the War! We Don't Want to Starve Any Longer':[1] German Working-class Women and the First World War

Helen Boak

In November 1915, Evelyn, Countess Blücher, an Englishwoman married to a Prussian aristocrat, wrote:

> But now the war has been going on for a year and a half, and it has not been possible to suppress the losses, the suffering, the horrors. The long lists of casualties have developed into great thick volumes; more and more men are being called up; women are realizing the enormous burden imposed upon them. They have to do the men's work as well as their own, and when they have earned their pay it all goes into the pockets of others who sell them food at enormous prices. Naturally they begin more than ever to say: 'Why should we work, starve, send our men out to fight? What is it all going to bring us? More work, more poverty, our men cripples, our homes ruined. What is it all for? ...The State which called upon us to fight cannot even give us decent food...'[2]

Blücher's diary entry came one month after the first food riots, over butter, were seen in several German cities, and food shortages and inequalities in food provisioning were to influence morale and attitudes towards the war and the government on the home front, especially among the working class. Although all German women shared the emotional trauma at the loss of a beloved husband, son, brother or fiancé at the front, it was to be Germany's working-class women who were to bear the brunt of the material deprivations, hardships, physical exploitation and sacrifices caused by the war though, even within the working class, a woman's war experience depended on her marital status and family circumstances; a young single woman who had to leave home to work in the munitions industry had a different experience from a mother with young children trying to eke out her Family War Benefit with homework, or from a woman whose husband was at home, one of over two million exempted workers, over one million of whom were fit for active service.[3] It is the purpose of this paper to explore German working-class women's experiences of the First World War.

In general, the German working class did not welcome the war; they were resigned to defending their nation and while we see pictures of women accompanying smiling soldiers off to war, many women wept openly as they waved their loved ones goodbye. In the last days of July thousands of working-class women had attended social democratic demonstrations for peace in 163 towns across Germany.[4] However, the agreement by the trades unions and the Social Democratic Party (SPD) on 4 August 1914 to be party to the 'civic peace' (Burgfrieden) proclaimed by the Kaiser, when all elements undertook to support this defensive war, and the measures put in place by the 24 Deputy Commanding Generals who under the Law of Siege were now responsible for administering the nation, ensured that women's opposition to the war was not only muted, but lacked leadership. Several leading SPD women faced imprisonment, censorship and speaking and agitation bans. The lack of leadership meant that working-class women's protest, in the first two years of the war arising out of grievances about food shortages and inequalities in food provisioning, took on the form of 'spontaneous outbreaks of militant self-help' on the streets, while from 1917 working women were also using the strike weapon, to hit industrial production in the factories.[5]

Family Welfare

For many working-class women, the war's first impact was financial, as husbands were called up or made unemployed, as were many working women as the economy shifted from peace-time production to war-time, and women were primarily employed in peace-time industries such as textiles. One young socialist wrote in his diary in early autumn 1914 of the situation in Hamburg's tenements: 'impoverished conditions, crying women, unemployment, despair'.[6] Some four million soldiers' wives, not all of whom came from the working class, were entitled to receive Family War Benefit, initially of 9 marks a month, with 6 marks per child.[7] It is clear that from the beginning Family War Benefit was insufficient to cater for a family which is why many towns supplemented it; local authorities had been ordered on 4 August 1914 to put in place welfare programmes to help all those 'who became needy because of the war', but these benefits were not uniform and were means tested.[8] Berlin gave soldiers' wives the same as the Family War Benefit so that the total benefit in Berlin amounted to 25 per cent of a skilled man's pre-war wage for a wife and child.[9] Across Germany, benefits varied in amount and kind and some industrial firms, such as Höchst in Frankfurt, also gave allowances to enlisted employees' families.[10] This inequality in the treatment of soldiers' wives and families was a cause of discontent. Many working-class soldiers' wives were forced to try and find employment, particularly in munitions and transport; 70 per cent of the married women working in the Bavarian arms industry in December 1916 were soldiers' wives. Some women found work with their husband's employer; a survey of 70 tram companies in November 1915 found that 20 per cent of their workforces were wives of enlisted men.[11] Some women undertook homework, for example, producing sandbags, gas masks and canvas straps for the army. In autumn 1916 an estimated 300,000 women were working from home but with the Hindenburg Programme's drive to mobilise all Germany's resources behind the war effort in late 1916, one army district managed to place 6,000 of its 10,000 homeworkers into munitions factories.[12] Although women were not conscripted under the Auxiliary Service Law of December 1916, a law of March 1917 withdrew Family War Benefit from any soldier's wife deemed capable of working, though she was allowed in some areas, as an incentive, to keep 50 per cent of her benefit.[13] In order to maximise the number of women in work and their output, the War Office created a special Women's Department in December 1916, replicated in all army districts, and headed by leading members of the middle-class women's movement which attempted *inter alia* to appoint factory nurses, improve the work environment, child care, and transport to and from work, and tried to arrange for workers to collect their ration cards and rationed food at more convenient times.[14] Belinda Davis notes that middle-class women were showing their patriotism by getting working-class women into war factories.[15]

Employment

No comprehensive statistics exist for women's employment during the First World War, and there are claims that two million, even five million more women were working.[16] Incomplete statistics show that it was to be summer 1916 before women's employment reached its pre-war level and it does seem that 1916/17 saw a substantial increase in women working. Once it became clear that the war would not be over by Christmas, women began to replace men in war-related industries from early 1915, once employer resistance had been overcome, and also in physically demanding work, sometimes outside, such as in construction, building roads, as grave-diggers, in slaughter-houses, and in the fire brigade. The female industrial workforce was predominantly single, unskilled or trained up to be semi-skilled, often having to take over heavy, physical work with no consideration given to women's ability to perform such work, and based in areas devoted to war-related industries. The number of women manual workers in Berlin increased by 172,000, in Düsseldorf by 97,000, for example. In one factory, only 500 of its 10,000 women workers came from the locality, and the others preferred to try and find accommodation in outlying areas, where they would share a bed on a 'Box and Cox' arrangement rather than stay in specially constructed barracks. As many of the women workers were unskilled, the turnover was acute; they moved if they found better working conditions, such as a canteen, work clothing, decent accommodation, and some consideration for a working mother's responsibilities. The head of the women's department in the Nuremberg War Office claimed that a turnover of one third was not uncommon. Some firms tried to employ the wives and daughters of former workers, believing they might have more loyalty to the firm.[17]

All labour protection laws had been lifted at the start of the war, and twelve hour shifts were the norm in industry, with some women doing double shifts, while 15 hours was the norm in the transport sector. It was not uncommon for women to pass out during the night shift – from exhaustion, hunger or illness and the number of accidents involving women rose but industrial incidents were subject to a news blackout.[18] Doctors were particularly concerned about the impact of night work and of work on pregnant and nursing women, many of whom were too weak to breastfeed their babies.[19] A marked deterioration in women's productivity was noted in the last two years of the war as women suffered not just under the physical demands that work in war-related industries and transportation, construction and mining made of them, but also from severe material deprivations. German officials calculated that over 763,000 Germans died as a direct result of the Allied blockade, but they failed to acknowledge the priority given to the Army in the allocation of food supplies and the mismanagement of food provisioning on the home front.[20]

Winter believes that female mortality rates in the first two years of the war differed little from pre-war figures, but after 1916 they rose exponentially; in 1918 they were double what might have been expected, with the age groups under 15 and over 60 particularly hard hit.[21] From 1917 onwards a deterioration in the health of the nation was clearly visible, with increases in stomach and intestinal illnesses. Between 1913 and 1918 the death rate from tuberculosis in towns with more than 15,000 inhabitants rose 91.1 per cent. The numbers dying of typhoid doubled between 1916 and 1917.[22] With regard to women, the numbers of women suffering from amenorrhea increased, as did complications in pregnancy. The birth rate declined substantially during the war, from 26.8 per 1,000 inhabitants in 1914 to 13.9 in 1917, and the babies being born were smaller and less heavy than before the war.[23]

Food Provisions

The German government had not planned for a long war. Germany was dependent on foreign imports for one-third of its foodstuffs as well as animal fodder. Food provisioning was a local responsibility and the authorities tried to use a system of price controls and rationing to ensure an equitable distribution of food at affordable prices.[24] Bread and potatoes were the staple of working-class families' diets and as early as October 1914 potatoes were being used in the making of bread, which became the first food to be rationed in February 1915. Throughout 1916 more staple foods were rationed – potatoes (April), butter and sugar (May), meat (June), eggs, milk and other fats (November). Women would collect their ration cards and newspapers would advise them of the amounts allowed, plus the time and place of sales, and they would begin to queue early, often bringing their folding chairs and knitting, to ensure they got something. If the shop sold out, they had to go elsewhere.[25] Eifert claims that in Berlin women would begin queueing at night and their older children would take their places in the morning to enable the women to go to work.[26] Queues, which became known as 'polonaises', had become a feature of city life in late 1915, and authorities were concerned that they became a hotbed of discontent, rumour and unrest. In October 1915 over 50 small riots involving thousands of women occurred in Berlin's working-class districts over butter – some protesting at the new higher price ceiling, others that a butter seller was holding back butter to sell to his wealthier customers.[27] In October and November 1915 there were also butter riots in Aachen, Cologne, Leipzig, Münster and Chemnitz.[28] Ethel Cooper, an Australian who spent the war in Leipzig, wrote to her sister on 24 October 1915 about the food riots in Chemnitz where the town hall and shops were stormed by people and, noting the huge increase in prices, she asked, 'What are the poor people to eat? ... Practically nothing but potatoes.'[29] Ethel Cooper could afford to get food from restaurants and throughout the war received food and hospitality from an English friend married to a German wool merchant, Connie Jaeger, who got food from their estate in the countryside and was able to trade it with merchants;

in December 1917, for example, she got 15 cwt of coal in exchange for 2 lbs of ham, but they had to store it in the bathroom because the cellar was broken into so often. Ethel noted that she could eat pheasant and pigeon, but had no sugar, flour or milk.[30] The necessities of life became luxuries.

Food Riots

The summer of 1916 saw a wave of food-related riots across Germany. Women would often march on town halls, demanding an increase and improvement in food supplies. Food riots continued at times of shortage throughout 1917, but now women helped themselves, and also physically attacked shopkeepers and market traders, so that some no longer brought their goods to market in working-class districts.[31] Working-class women were dependent on obtaining their families' rations; they did not have the money to buy goods on the flourishing black market, nor to buy in dried goods to hoard. They had little opportunity to produce food for themselves – on balconies, or in gardens, keeping goats, rabbits and hens or growing vegetables - and so, if they did not have relatives in the countryside from whom they could obtain food, they were reduced to hamstering - travelling into the countryside on a Sunday to barter, buy or steal from rural producers, though they ran the risk of having the food confiscated by inspectors at railway stations on their return.[32] As the war went on women resorted to looting or stealing. The numbers of women convicted of crimes against property doubled between 1913 and 1917.[33] Many believed that they had to resort to criminality to survive. As Ethel Cooper noted: 'where everything is forbidden, you simply have to break the laws to go on living'.[34] In June 1918, Connie Jaeger was outraged to discover that the porter's wife had been stealing potatoes from the cellar. Cooper noted that 'the experiences of the last four years have made that woman feel that she has a perfect right to steal from the rich'.[35]

In an attempt to ensure that people had access to at least one meal a day, the government ordered local authorities in summer 1916 to extend their provision of soup kitchens. By October 1916 357 of 530 towns with over 10,000 inhabitants had 1,458 kitchens providing 'mass feeding'.[36] The use of soup kitchens tended to vary with the availability of food supplies. During the winter of 1916-17, the so-called turnip winter when the turnip replaced the potato as the staple food, more and more people overcame their reluctance – soup kitchens had poor relief connotations – and used the soup kitchen. In Hamburg six million portions were served in April 1917, and even towards the war's end, some 20 per cent of its population got a meal from a soup kitchen.[37] In late 1916, with the drive now on to mobilise all Germany's resources behind the war effort, the government increased the ration allocations of meat, flour and butter for workers in heavy industry, which included female munitions workers.[38] Women in the last three months of pregnancy also got extra rations, including full milk, to which children under six were also entitled, but pregnant women's right to go to the head of the queue for milk was withdrawn in 1917 in response to popular feeling; they were considered selfish, removing their labour and creating an extra mouth to feed.[39] By summer 1917 rations amounted to about 1,000 calories a day, and were about 40 per cent of pre-war intake.[40] However, the rations were not always available; in the winter of 1916-17 weeks went by without potatoes because of the poor harvest and transportation difficulties and the turnip was used extensively as a replacement; it, too, was rationed. During the war over 11,000 substitute foodstuffs were approved and they were of dubious nutritional value.[41]

It was not just hunger that afflicted the working class. The winter of 1916-17 was the coldest in living memory, with temperatures of -24°F. Water pipes, food and rivers all froze, hindering the transportation of food and coal. There was a coal shortage and public buildings such as public baths, schools, and theatres were closed, transport services reduced, street lights dimmed and gas and electricity were rationed.[42] The deputy commanding generals noted that 'the population won't go along with another winter without sufficient coal. To starve and to freeze is just too much.'[43] The lack of soap impacted on public health, personnel hygiene and laundry. Clothes were rationed in August 1916, shoes in December 1916 and cloth shoes with wooden soles became the norm, with children going barefoot in summer.[44] Newspapers were used to line coats, as even old recycled clothes were rationed.[45] By the war's end working-class Germans were quite literally walking round in rags.

Turnip Winter

By the end of 1916, following the battles of Verdun and the Somme, the mood among the working class, according to Jean Quataert, 'had turned sullen, focused on the fate of family members at the front'.[46] War weariness was setting in among broad sections of the population, with increasing annoyance among the working class at the injustices and inequalities in the supply of food, and with the turnip winter of 1916/17 Chickering claims that 'consensus had broken down about both the distribution of sacrifice and the legitimacy of the war'.[47] Women were to be found in large numbers in the strikes that hit German industry in spring 1917 and January 1918. The initial impetus for strikes in 1917 which affected the Ruhr, the Rhineland, Hamburg, Kiel, Nuremberg and Berlin, was often food-related but increasingly, political demands were also being made, such as the reform of the suffrage laws, the lifting of the state of siege, the freeing of political prisoners, and peace. In 1916, 437 firms had been hit by strike action, in 1917, 3,392 with some 1.5 million strikers calling for improved food provisions, higher wages to meet the rises in inflation, and political reform.[48] The late January 1918 strike wave was the largest in the history of Wilhelmine Germany, with over one million workers participating. Once again, the demands related to improved food supplies, and an end to the war. In Berlin, 400,000 munitions workers – some say mostly women – downed tools and strikes were experienced in Hamburg, Kiel, Nuremberg and Munich.[49] Some historians have seen the strikes during January and February 1918 as a turning point in the war on the home front, an indication of how Germans no longer believed in an ultimate German victory, and, increasingly dissatisfied, were willing to protest.[50]

The SPD continued its support for the war, albeit grudgingly, but not even the improved harvest of 1917, the defeat of Russia and the initial successes in the offensive in the West could overcome war weariness. In the summer of 1918 the deputy commanding generals noted a change of mood, particularly among 'working women, especially family women', who were now aware that the separate peace with Russia had brought no improvement in the food situation. At the end of August four meat-free weeks in September and October were declared.[51] In Munich women demanded that the Bavarian government declare peace and provide food and in their letters to the front women called upon husbands and sons to come home, but it was to be a military mutiny, of sailors in Kiel, that was to spark the revolution.[52] But the peace did not bring much easing in the food crisis and transport became even more difficult, particularly in areas which were occupied. It was to be July 1919 before the blockade was lifted and some price controls and rationing of various foodstuffs remained in place until 1922.[53] In 1921 a million children a day were fed in the food kitchens run by the Quakers in 1,640 German communities.[54] Poverty remained the urban poor's constant companion.

As Peter Fritzsche has noted, 'what is extraordinary is how long the German people put up with the hardships of war'.[55] Both Ethel Cooper and Princess Blücher believed the Germans were a subservient, passive and obedient people, accepting all regulations without demur. 'I do believe that if they were bidden to go out and eat grass, they would obey in herds', wrote Princess Blücher and Ethel Cooper referred to them as sheep.[56] In February 1919 Princess Blücher noted, however, her admiration for the 'misguided and battered people whose heroism and self-sacrifice have often verged on the super-human'.[57] The bulk of this super-human effort had come from Germany's working class, particularly its women.

Notes

1. Belinda Davis, *Home Fires Burning: Food, Politics, and Everyday Life in World War 1 Berlin* (Chapel Hill, 2000), pp.223-24.
2. Evelyn, Princess Blücher, *An English Wife in Berlin* (New York, 1920), p.94.
3. Richard Bessel, *Germany after the First World War* (Oxford, 1993), p.13.
4. Heinz Hagenlücke, 'The home front in Germany', in John Bourne, Peter Liddle and Ian Whitehead (eds), *The Great World War 1914-45; Vol. 2. The people's experience* (London, 2001), p.72.
5. Volker Ullrich, 'Everyday Life and the German Working Class, 1914-1918', in Roger Fletcher (ed.), *Bernstein to Brandt: A Short History of German Social Democracy* (London, 1987), p.60.
6. Peter Fritzsche, *Germans into Nazis* (London, 1998), p.32.
7. Birthe Kundrus, *Kriegerfrauen. Familienpolitik und Geschlechterverhältnisse im Ersten und Zweiten Weltkrieg* (Hamburg, 1995), p.51.
8. Larry Frohman, *Poor Relief and Welfare in Germany from the Reformation to World War 1* (Cambridge, 2008), pp.215, 217.
9. Ute Daniel, 'Funktionalisierung von Frauen und Familien in der Kriegswirtschaft 1914-1918 – Tendenzen und Gegentendenzen', in Vorbreitungsgruppe Historikerinnentreffen 1983, *Dokumentation 4. Historikerinnen-Treffen* (Berlin, 1983), p.31.
10. Christoph Regulski, *Klippfisch und Steckrüben* (Frankfurt am Main, 2012), p.39.
11. Bessel, op.cit., p.20.
12. Marie-Elisabeth Lüders, *Das unbekannte Heer* (Berlin, 1936), p.146.
13. Landesarchiv Berlin, BRep 235, HLA MF 2740, letter from the Reich Chancellery to several women's organisations, 14 August 1917.
14. Daniel, 'Funktionalisierung', p.35.
15. Davis, op.cit., pp.172-3.

16. Sabine Hering, *Die Kriegsgewinnlerinnen: Praxis und Ideologie der deutschen Frauenbewegung im Ersten Weltkrieg* (Pfaffenweiler, 1990), pp.76, 143.

17. Lüders, op.cit., pp.86-7, 155-6, 190-4; Daniel, 'Funktionalisierung', p.44.

18. Ullrich, op. cit., p.59.

19. Lüders, op.cit., pp.178, 212.

20. *Gewerkschaftliche Frauenzeitung*, Vol.4, No.3 (12 February, 1919), p.23; Peter Lummel, 'Food Provisioning in the German Army in the First World War', in Ina Zweiniger-Bargielowska, Rachel Duffett and Alain Drouard (eds), *Food and War in Twentieth Century Europe* (Farnham, 2011), pp.13-25.

21. Jay Winter, 'Some paradoxes of the First World War', in Richard Wall and Jay Winter (eds), *The Upheaval of War: Family, Work and Welfare in Europe, 1914-1918* (Cambridge, 1988), p.30.

22. Regulski, op. cit., p.260.

23. Helen Boak, *Women in the Weimar Republic* (Manchester, 2013), p.32.

24. Hans-Jürgen Teuteberg, 'Food Provisioning on the German Home Front, 1914-1918', in Zweiniger-Bargielowska, Duffett and Drouard (eds), op. cit., pp.59-72.

25. Ibid., pp.63, 66.

26. Christiane Eifert, 'Frauenarbeit im Krieg. Die Berliner "Heimatfront" 1914-1918', *Internationale wissenschaftliche Korrespondenz zur Geschichte der deutschen Arbeiterbewegung*, Vol.21, No.3 (September 1985), p.290.

27. Davis, op.cit., p.80.

28. Richard J Evans, *Sozialdemokratie und Frauenemanzipation im deutschen Kaiserreich* (Berlin, 1979), p.299.

29. Decie Denholm, *Behind the Lines: One Woman's War 1914-18* (London, 1982), p.107.

30. Ibid., pp.165, 233.

31. Davis, op. cit., pp.211-12.

32. Daniel, 'Funktionalisierung', p.49.

33. Ute Daniel, 'The Politics of Rationing versus the Politics of Subsistence: Working-Class Women in Germany, 1914-1918', in Fletcher (ed.), op. cit., p.92.

34. Denholm, op.cit., p.270.

35. Ibid., p.260.

36. Kundrus, op.cit., p.138.

37. Roger Chickering, *Imperial Germany and the Great War, 1914-1918* (Cambridge, 3rd ed., 2014), p.166; Keith Allen, 'Food and the German Home Front: Evidence from Berlin', in Gail Braybon (ed.), *Evidence, History and the Great War: Historians and the Impact of 1914-18* (Oxford, 2003), p.178.

38. Teuteberg, op. cit., p.63; Davis, op. cit., p.159.

39. Ibid., pp.165-66.

40. Boak, op. cit., p.27.

41. Davis, op. cit., pp.204-6.

42. Denholm, op.cit., pp.178-81.

43. Davis, op.cit., p.209.

44. Blücher, op. cit., pp.233; Elizabeth H. Tobin, 'War and the Working Class: The Case of Düsseldorf 1914-1918', *Central European History*, Vol.13, No.3/4 (1985), pp.291-2.

45. Roger Chickering, *The Great War and Urban Life in Germany* (Cambridge, 2007), pp.276-78.

46. Jean Quataert, 'Women's Wartime Services under the Cross: Patriotic Communities in Germany, 1912-1918', in Roger Chickering and Stig Förster (eds), *Great War, Total War: Combat and Mobilization on the Western Front, 1914-1918* (Cambridge, 2000), p.466.

47. Chickering, *The Great War*, p.459.

48. Regulski, op. cit., pp.197-98.

49. Sabine Hering, 'Krieg dem Kriege', *Ariadne*, Vol.17 (March 1990), p.33.

50. Regulski, op. cit., pp.270-71.

51. Ibid., p.289.

52. Davis, op.cit., p.230.

53. Boak, op. cit., p.227.

54. http://www.quakersintheworld.org/quakers-in-action/302, accessed 29 November, 2014.

55. Fritzsche, op.cit., p.74.

56. Denholm, op. cit., p.134; Blücher, op. cit., pp.176-77.

57. Ibid., p.328.

Clara Zetkin and the British Anti-War Movement

John S. Partington

Clara Zetkin was a prominent women's leader of the Social Democratic Party of Germany (SPD) from 1878 to 1917, the founder of the Socialist Women's International (SWI) in 1907, a leading figure in the Spartacist Movement from 1915 to 1919, the women's leader of the Independent Social Democratic Party of Germany (USPD) between 1917 and 1920 and the leader of the Communist Women's International from 1920 until her death in 1933. She also had a long relationship with the British socialist and labour movements. In 1896 she attended the London Congress of the Second International as an SPD delegate, working with Sidney Webb on education policy. In 1909 she visited London as a guest of both the Adult Suffrage Society (ASS) and the Social Democratic Party (SDP), speaking on the suffrage question at Holborn Town Hall and addressing the May Day rally in Hyde Park from the international platform.

As editor of the international socialist women's journal, *Die Gleichheit* (Equality), Zetkin was the main link between socialist women around the world. She also published widely in the national presses of many countries, including Britain. She was reported in the British press from 1889 onwards and published her first article, a May Day greeting from the SPD, in *Justice*, the journal of the Social Democratic Federation (SDF), in 1899.

The Second Boer War

Her first public comment in Britain on the subject of war, however, appeared a year later in a letter to the editor of *Justice* entitled 'May Greetings from Stuttgart'. In this she praised the SDF for its principled opposition to the war in South Africa:

> Wherever on the first of May the working class cries to capitalist society: 'Peace on Earth! Fraternity between the nations! War against war!' their thoughts and sympathies will turn towards that gallant little body of Socialist fighters in England, which dares to oppose the Socialist ideals and revendications to a world of power, of prejudice and of misled passions, roused by the present criminal war.[1]

Later that same year, at the 1900 Paris Congress of the Second International, Zetkin again raised the issue of the war in South Africa, this time condemning British imperial policy in the context of other contemporary atrocities. As *Justice* reports it,

> Clara Zetkin [...] then proposed a resolution condemning with indignation the savage policy adopted by the Russian despotism towards the Finns and the Poles, 'the atrocities of the English Government towards the Boers of South Africa,' and the cruelties and massacres committed by the Turks in Armenia.[2]

The Extraordinary International Socialist Congress, Basel

As tensions rose within Europe during the first decade or so of the twentieth century, Zetkin remained keen to promote socialist opposition to international conflict. With the outbreak of war in the Balkans in 1912 the International Socialist Bureau called the Extraordinary International Socialist Peace Congress in Basel, Switzerland. Although it had been customary from 1907 for Zetkin to organise socialist women's conferences ahead of each socialist congress, time was against her on this occasion so she urged, in letters to the chief British socialist newspapers (*The Clarion*, the *Daily Herald*, the *Labour Leader*, *Justice* and the *League Leaflet*), male comrades to ensure a fair representation of women were delegated to Basel. As she wrote in *The Clarion* and elsewhere to her British readership,

> This powerful meeting must show that in all countries Socialist women are united with the workers and the Socialist Parties in waging war against war. [...] Women who have worked and wept refuse to give up their loved ones to be shamelessly and callously slaughtered through the frenzy of military and Imperialist factions.[3]

Although Zetkin objected to male socialist comrades being killed in international conflicts, she was not a pacifist. She took a principled anti-militarist stand but was conscious that, in the struggle for the socialist revolution, blood may have to be shed. Reporting Zetkin's speech to the Basel peace congress, *Justice* quoted her thus:

> But, if we Socialist women and mothers rise against the wholesale slaughter, [...] it is not to say that we would not be courageous enough to make great sacrifices for the sake of great ideals. We have gone through the hard school of life under capitalism, and have become fighters. And we will not hesitate to see our loved ones fight and fall if it be for the cause of freedom. In that struggle we will be

filled with the spirit of those mothers of old who handed the shield to their sons with the words: 'Return either with it or upon it'.[4] Thus, although one might consider Zetkin's oft-used expression 'war against war' as a broad metaphor for opposition to military conflict – a phrase which represents all acts of antiwar protest – it is clear that Zetkin was prepared to contemplate the need for violence to defeat capitalist aggression and transform society into the socialism which she anticipated.

The Great War

With the coming of the so-called Great War, Zetkin remained the secretary of the SWl. While the majority SPD endorsed the German government's war policy, she, along with Karl Liebknecht, Rosa Luxemburg and Franz Mehring, declared, in a letter dated 10 September and published in the Zurich *Volksrecht* newspaper, her opposition to the war. This letter was subsequently published in *Justice* on 12 November and reprinted in the *Merthyr Pioneer* nine days later.[5] While before the war her political objectives ranged from issues such as adult suffrage, the political and industrial organisation of women and anti-militarism, during the Great War her concerns were narrowed to propagandising for peace and ensuring non-combatants had a basic standard of living. Within the context of her anti-militarism, she persisted in her advocacy of international socialist fraternity. She considered the war to be rooted in capitalist competition and imperial rivalries for which the working classes of all countries were blameless. Although Zetkin had previously been strongly opposed to socialists cooperating with bourgeois organisations even where their goals might appear similar (her opposition to the British suffragettes being a case in point), during the Great War she moderated this position, reporting in *Justice* in November 1914 that in Germany, 'the Socialist women are working peacefully alongside the bourgeois nationalist "Women's Service," and also with its representatives on communal bodies, without however joining its organisation, which would be a drag upon them in their work'.[6]

Zetkin's conciliatory attitude towards bourgeois organisations was further demonstrated in December of the same year when she published a letter in *Jus Suffragii*, the monthly journal of the bourgeois International Woman Suffrage Alliance. Here Zetkin began to spell out her principles on the postwar settlement:

> All nations have a right to national independence equal to that which Germany has won for itself. Let us raise our voices loud and fearlessly for peace as soon as our people have gained this object ... for a peace which binds neighbouring nations to us,

instead of a policy of conquest by force, which creates the incentive for future combat.[7]

Concerned about the potential for the war to cause divisions between nations *post-bellum*, she asserted, 'The blood of dead and wounded must not become a stream to divide what present need and future hope unite. It must be a chain to bind eternally'.[8]

As avenues of communication between German and British socialists improved (using Swiss and Dutch comrades as conduits), the *Labour Leader* was able to publish several 'official messages' from German socialist leaders on 31 December 1914. In her piece (which was also printed in the *Merthyr Pioneer*), Zetkin not only praises the work of the Independent Labour Party (ILP) in pursuing an antiwar policy, she also foreshadows the fate of the discredited Second International, the main parties of which fell behind their national governments on the outbreak of the war. She writes, 'the international solidarity and brotherhood of the workers cannot be killed. It lives as long as Capitalist exploitation and bondage is the fate of the workers of all nations. When, over ruins and ashes, the third International shall arise, the glorious attitude of the ILP will shine like a guiding star'.[9] This reference to a 'third international', the first of several by Zetkin during the war, predating the policy of Lenin's Zimmerwald Congress by nine months, demonstrates both Zetkin's acknowledgement that the prewar Second International was irredeemable but also her desire for international socialism to re-emerge at an institutional level.

International Socialist Women's Peace Conference, Bern

In condemning the Second International and advocating a third, Zetkin was not severing all ties with prewar international socialism. On the contrary, she saw her own SWI as the key bridge betwixt pre- and postwar international organisation. During the early months of 1915 she worked with comrades abroad to strengthen the network of socialist sisterhood and – while international correspondence remained important – physical proximity became crucial in Zetkin's campaign. A foretaste of things to come was announced in the March 1915 issue of *Labour Woman* by Mary Longman, the secretary of the British section of the SWI:

> The letters we have lately received from abroad all discuss the possibility of an International Conference of Socialist Women shortly meeting in some neutral country. [...] the Women's International Council has written to correspondents abroad

suggesting that we could come together and discuss what we can do to bring about a [']just and lasting peace.'[10]

According to reports in *Labour Woman*, the British section of the SWI was crucial in making the desired conference a reality. Thus, the April editorial, revealing the conference to have been an achieved fact, notes that,

> A letter received here from Frau Clara Zetkin gives as the starting point from which to write of this reassembly of women Socialists. In this letter, Clara Zetkin tells us of the joy with which she received a message from the British women, expressing the hope that a meeting would take place. It came (she said) 'like a sunbeam at night'.[11]

The gathering of the SWI peace conference took place from 26-28 March 1915 in Bern. As the *Labour Woman* editorial explains,

> Four representatives of the movement in this country left London to meet the Socialist women of other countries: Miss Mary Longman (Women's Labour League), Dr [Marion] Phillips (Women's International Council, British Section), Mrs Ada Salter and Miss Margaret Bondfield (ILP, and Women's Trade Union League). They met Clara Zetkin a day or two before the conference was held, to put the business into shape.[12]

Although Longman was initially nervous about meeting German delegates, stressing that 'There must be no harbouring of revengeful feelings' and suggesting that 'there are certain vexed questions which it would be necessary to avoid',[13] in fact no subject was avoided during discussions and the press was unanimous in declaring 'Cordial Relations Between British and German Delegates'.[14]

The conference established the policies upon which socialist women would campaign back in their home countries and, according to the Dundee *Courier*,

> A general resolution was adopted which referred to the Capitalist and Imperialist origins of the war and its terrible effects, especially for the workers of the different nations involved. It called for a speedy ending of the war by a peace which would expiate the wrong done to Belgium, impose no humiliating conditions on any nation, and would recognise the right of all nationalities, large and small, to independence and self-government.[15]

Furthermore, the *Courier* noted that 'Two additions to the first draft were made on the proposal of the British delegates. The first dealt with the menace of the armament interests and their huge international organisation. The second dealt with the high prices charged for food and fuel and the extortions of contractors.'[16]

German Socialist Anti-War Manifesto

Whilst the socialist women were coming together to expound an international policy, the *Labour Leader* was publicising the manifesto of the Anti-War Group within the SPD which included Karl Lieb-knecht, Georg Ledebour, Otto Rühle, Franz Mehring, Clara Zetkin and Rosa Luxemburg. That manifesto demanded,

> a peace based on the principles laid down unanimously at the International Socialist Congresses at Copenhagen and Basle and accepted by the German delegates. The chief of these principles are:
> NO ANNEXATIONS.
> POLITICAL AND ECONOMIC INDEPENDENCE OF EVERY NATION.
> DISARMAMENT.
> COMPULSORY ARBITRATION.[17]

In addition, the conference declared: 'We demand the publication of the terms on which the Governments are ready to make peace'.[18]

Conclusion

As is clear, the growing German opposition to the war was in tune with the SWI. It was the mood expressed by such groups as these that inspired Zetkin, in a letter to *Labour Woman* in May 1916, to declare: 'A time will come – perhaps sooner than we think – when the workers in their multitudes will write across the streams of blood in a third International'.[19] Although Zetkin remained an important figure in the British socialist press throughout the rest of the war, increased censorship in Germany, her departure from the SPD, and a period of imprisonment, made it difficult for her to engage in new initiatives. Nonetheless, the Bern conference succeeded in welding a spirit of international solidarity between socialist women and their activities contributed to the socialists in Britain, Germany and elsewhere gradually extricating themselves from their pro-war governments and developing independent policies for the postwar world.

Notes

1. Clara Zetkin, 'May greetings from Stuttgart', *Justice*, 12 May 1900, p.6.
2. 'The international congress', *Justice*, 6 October 1900, pp.2-3 (p.3).
3. Zetkin 'War against war. To the socialist women of all countries', *The Clarion*, 22 November 1912, p.6.
4. 'Socialist women and the international demonstration at Basel', *Justice*, 14 December 1912, p.6.
5. See Karl Liebknecht, Rosa Luxemburg, Franz Mehring and Zetkin, 'The German SDP and the war', *Volksrecht*, 31 October 1914, rpt in *Justice*, 12 November 1914, p.1; and Karl Liebknecht, Rosa Luxemburg, Franz Mehring and Zetkin, 'Another bubble bursts', *Volksrecht*, 31 October 1914, rpt in *Merthyr Pioneer*, 21 November, p.3.
6. Zetkin, 'The duty of working women in war-time', *Justice*, 19 November 1914, p.2.
7. Zetkin, 'Clara Zetkin on the war', *Jus Suffragii*, 1 December 1914, pp.206-07 (p.206).
8. Zetkin, 'Clara Zetkin on the war', p.207.
9. Zetkin, 'German socialists want peace. Official message to the "Labour Leader". Clara Zetkin', *Labour Leader*, 31 December 1914, pp.1-2 (p.2).
10. Mary Longman, 'Our sisters abroad', *Labour Woman*, 2.11, March 1915, p.282.
11. 'Women's war against war. Towards the new socialist international', *Labour Woman*, 2.12, April 1915, pp.285-86 (p.285).
12. 'Women's war against war', p.285.
13. Longman, 'Our sisters abroad', p.282.
14. 'Women socialists of European nations meet at international conference in Switzerland. Cordial relations between German and British delegates', *The Courier* [Dundee], 6 April 1915, p.7. See also 'Women socialists meet. Harmony at Berne conference which calls for expiation to Belgium', *New York Times*, 17 April 1915.
15. 'Women socialists of European nations meet at international conference in Switzerland', p.7.
16. 'Women socialists of European nations meet at international conference in Switzerland', p.7.
17. 'Manifesto of German socialists. A call for a united peace movement. The slaughter of the people must cease', *Labour Leader*, 13.12, 1 April 1915, p.1.
18. 'Manifesto of German socialists', p.1.
19. Zetkin, 'The women's international. A message for women's day in Holland from Clara Zetkin (international secretary)', *Labour Woman*, 4.1, May 1916, pp.4-5 (p.5).

Notes on Contributors

Ian Birchall

Ian is a socialist writer and translator. For many years he taught at Middlesex Polytechnic. He is the author of *The Spectre of Babeuf* (1997); *Sartre Against Stalinism* (2004); *A Rebel's Guide to Lenin* (2005); *Tony Cliff: A Marxist For His Time* (2011). Ian has translated Alfred Rosmer and Victor Serge, and published numerous articles in political and academic journals. He is on the Editorial Board of *Revolutionary History* and is a member of the London Socialist Historians Group and the SHS. He has a very interesting website: http://grimanddim.org/about/

Helen Boak

Dr Helen Boak was formerly Head of History at the University of Hertfordshire. She has written numerous essays on the history of women in early 20th century German politics and society. Helen is the author of *Women in the Weimar Republic* (Manchester University Press, 2013). Several of Helen Boak's articles can be found on the Academia.edu platform: http://independent.academia.edu/HelenBoak

Duncan Bowie

Duncan Bowie is a member of the SHS committee and of the committee of the London Labour Housing Group. He is a lecturer at the University of Westminster. He is the author of SHS OP No 34, *Roots of the British Socialist Movement*. Duncan is also the author of *The Radical and Socialist Tradition in British Planning: From Puritan Colonies to Garden Cities* (Ashgate, 2015) and *Politics, Planning and Homes in a World City* (Routledge, 2010).

Keith Laybourn

Keith Laybourn has been Diamond Jubilee Professor of the University of Huddersfield since April 2012. He is the author and editor of 47 books on aspects of labour movement history, women and unemployment in 20th century Britain, philanthropy, working-class gambling, and policing in Britain during the inter-war years. His most recent book is *Marxism in Britain: Dissent, Decline and Re-emergence 1945-c.2000* (Routledge, 2015). Keith's early research was on the Labour Party and the Independent Labour Party. Keith Laybourn is President of the Society for the Study of Labour History.

John S Partington

Dr John S Partington works for Network Rail and is an independent historian. He has written or edited *Building Cosmopolis: The Political Thought of H G Wells* (2003), *Clara Zetkin: National and International Contexts* (with Marilyn J Boxer, SHS OP No 31, 2012) and *The Life, Music and Thought of Woody Guthrie: A Critical Appraisal* (2011). He has written extensively on the work of novelist H G Wells. John is currently researching the reception and influence of Clara Zetkin on British politics. He has a lively blog: http://drjohnspartington.blogspot.co.uk/

The Socialist History Society

The Socialist History Society was founded in 1992 and includes many leading Socialist and labour historians, academic and amateur researchers, in Britain and overseas. The SHS holds regular events, public meeting controversies. We produce a range of publications, including the journal *Socialist History* and a regular Newsletter.

The SHS is the successor to the Communist Party History Group, which was established in 1946 and is now totally independent of all political parties and groups. We are engaged in and seek to encourage historical studies from a Marxist and broadly-defined left perspective. We are interested in all aspects of human history from the earliest social formations to the present day and aim for an international approach.

We are particularly interested in the various struggles of labour, of women, of progressive campaigns and peace movements around the world, as well as the history of colonial peoples, black people, and all oppressed communities seeking justice, human dignity and liberation.

Each year we produce two issues of our journal *Socialist History*, one or two historical pamphlets in our *Occasional Publications* series, and frequent members' Newsletters. We hold public lectures and seminars mainly in London. In addition, we hold special conferences, book launches and joint events with other friendly groups.

Join the Socialist History Society today!

Members receive all our serial publications for the year at no extra cost and regular mailings about our activities. Members can vote at our AGM and seek election to positions on the committee, and are encouraged to participate in other society activities.

Annual membership fees for 2016 (renewable every January):

Full UK	£25.00
Concessionary UK	£18.00
Europe full	£30.00
Europe concessionary	£24.00
Rest of world full	£35.00
Rest of world concessionary	£29.00

For details of institutional subscriptions, please e-mail the treasurer on francis@socialisthistorysociety.co.uk.

To join the society for 2016, please send your name and address plus a cheque/PO payable to **Socialist History Society** to: SHS, 50 Elmfield Road, Balham, London SW17 8AL. You can also pay online.

Visit our websites on www.socialisthistorysociety.co.uk and www.socialist-history-journal.org.uk.